PROFESSIONAL PREPARATION IN ATHLETIC TRAINING

PROCEEDINGS OF THE PROFESSIONAL PREPARATION CONFERENCES: NATIONAL ATHLETIC TRAINERS ASSOCIATION

Nashville, Tennessee
January 7-9, 1979

Nashville, Tennessee
January 4-6, 1980

Palo Alto, California
February 15-17, 1980

HUMAN KINETICS PUBLISHERS
CHAMPAIGN, ILLINOIS

Publications Director: Richard D. Howell

Editor: Margery Brandfon

Typesetter: Sandra Meier

Text Design and Layout: Denise Peters and Lezli Harris

Library of Congress Catalog Card Number: 82-81094

ISBN: 0-931250-32-3

Edited by: Gerald W. Bell
             University of Illinois at Urbana-Champaign

Published by: HUMAN KINETICS PUBLISHERS, INC.
                Box 5076   Champaign, IL 61820

TABLE OF CONTENTS

v

PART THREE. PREVENTING ATHLETIC INJURIES THROUGH HEALTH AND FITNESS

PART FOUR. LIABILITY AND MANAGEMENT

PREFACE

This publication represents a collection of papers presented at the National Athletic Trainers Association Professional Preparation Conferences, January 7-9, 1979, and January 4-6, 1980, in Nashville, Tennessee, and February 15-17, 1980, in Palo Alto, California. Coordinated and conducted by the NATA Professional Education Committee, these conferences featured presentations by nationally known athletic trainers, physicians, and other sports medicine professionals from throughout the United States. Presented in this publication are papers representing several major subject matter areas in athletic training, including Athletic Training in Higher Education (Part One), Athletic Injuries (Part Two), Preventing Athletic Injuries Through Health and Fitness (Part Three), and Liability and Management (Part Four).

The editor wishes to thank the NATA Board of Directors and the Professional Education Committee for their support and encouragement throughout this project. Appreciation is also extended to Della Ranslem, typist, and to Jeff Dooley and Barbara Bell, proofreaders, for their valuable assistance in preparation of this publication.

Gerald W. Bell

PART ONE

ATHLETIC TRAINING IN HIGHER EDUCATION

Athletic Training Education at the Crossroads

Sayers Miller
The Pennsylvania State University

Athletic training and education today are at a crossroads; we are reaching a point where we must make a decision about where we are going with athletic training education. But before we can discuss the future of athletic training, we must understand its past.

For the last 20 years, the National Athletic Trainer's Association (NATA) has been the official approving body for direction of athletic training curricula. In 1959, the first athletic training education program was approved by the NATA Board of Directors. This program set up guidelines for individuals wanting to professionally prepare themselves for a career in athletic training.

In 1969, a procedure was developed for approving educational programs. Today, that procedure is almost intact. A lot of other things have happened since then. By 1979, 52 schools were offering athletic training curricula; 48 of these are undergraduate curricula, 7 graduate curricula, and 3 offer both undergraduate and graduate curricula. Also, the number of actual curricula that professionally prepare faculty-trainers for the high school level has increased. Finally, this professional preparation conference has occurred in addition to other educational aspects due to the efforts of the special professional education subcommittee.

Another milestone in NATA's history is that today we have the first approved program for the athletic trainer to obtain Continuing Education Units (CEUs required starting January 1, 1980). This is one of the first programs the NATA has developed enabling certified athletic trainers to fulfill CEU requirements. We have provided educational programs for athletic trainers, and with this continuing education, we hope

Until his untimely death in 1980, Sayers Miller, MS, RPT, ATC, was NATA curriculum director and trainer at The Pennsylvania State University in University Park, Pennsylvania.

to not only prevent obsolescence from creeping into the field, but to grow and flourish. Through professional education and preparation, we hope to keep abreast of the knowledge we must have.

Other types of educational programs have been proposed and studied. Guidelines, and in a few cases, some experimental programs have been established. One such program is the high school faculty-trainer instructional programs offered by the Northwestern University and the state of North Carolina. Other areas the Professional Education Committee is considering are establishing athletic training as a major field of study, not as a minor like the 48 programs existing today, and having athletic training curricula offered by other departments like the Allied Health Department. Also, we have worked on guidelines for junior colleges' curriculum to upgrade present educational programs. These ongoing projects of the Professional Education Committee must still be discussed and researched before they can blossom.

The next thing we need to examine is the teacher-trainer curricula in order to find patterns in each that could give us information about the quality of our curricula. One place we want to look and study is the certification exams. How are the curriculum graduates performing on the certification exam? Individual scores indicate that many of our curriculum graduates are scoring high on the written part of their exam, not as high as physical therapy school graduates, but higher than those in the other routes to certification. Although there is little statistical difference between the varying routes to certification, a larger percentage of graduates from the teacher-trainer curricula are failing either parts of or the entire certification exam. Naturally, this raises questions about the quality of the teacher-trainer curricula. Do these findings indicate weaknesses in the guidelines that have established the curricula, or have certain curricula pulled down the rest? We still don't have the answer because, as yet, we do not have a statistically significant trend.

How do we compare the data on experimental programs (faculty-trainer) with other types of educational programs? Although we have one type of experimental program, we have not yet had graduates from it. Thus, because we lack sufficient numbers by which to judge the program, the certification exam cannot provide many answers about trends in our experimental programs. Some trends, however, have been noted by not only the Professional Education Committee, but by program directors and those interested in athletic training education, and it is these trends that will be discussed next.

One important area of concern is providing students with background in such basic sciences as anatomy and physiology. In fact, curriculum graduates score lowest on these two sciences on their certification exam. Whether we even need this background is something to be analyzed; nevertheless our programs, which are housed in health and/or physical education departments, are weak in anatomy or physiology. Some of the requirements are fulfilled by combined courses, but our guidelines for the curriculum have been changed to allow students to take a combined course only if the amount of time spent in the course is comparable to two courses. Many curricula have added a second course to reinforce the anatomy and physiology. Some curricula are fortunate to be connected with medical schools or allied health fields like physical therapy, occupational therapy, and medical technology, where they have been able to offer human cadaver courses, thereby benefiting students. As stated previously, however, the anatomy and physiology areas in most of our programs are weak and need to be strengthened.

Another area needing considerable improvement is the clinical experience. Some believe more hours of clinical experience are needed; however, this is a hotly debated issue because most health and education departments think that the current 600-hour requirement is ridiculous in the first place. Most of these departments are only attuned to education-type programs such as student teaching. Credit for such experience is restricted by limitations like no more than 20 hours of clinical experience for one credit and various credit hour formulas. Athletic training clinical experience, however, cannot be compared to any other type of clinical experience. For example, experience in student teaching is a set type of experience. You know that on a certain day you are going to teach 20 or 30 students and you are going to teach a certain lesson plan. This is not comparable to clinical experience in the training room, on the field, or on a trip. A physical therapy clinical experience, which provides regulated experiences where you know you are going to have a patient here, there, etc., also is not comparable to athletic training clinical experience. With physical therapy experience, you may have athletic injuries or other chronic patient problems. Looking at it from such aspects as prevention, evaluation, or treatment, more and more hours of experience are needed, not only for the athlete and the injury, but for those people involved with sports. Increasing athletic training clinical experience is a battle worth fighting for. Having seen curricula around the country, I have found that most of them far exceed the 600 hours in their actual requirement. Thus, I would encourage increasing the clinical experience hours for students.

Also, the clinical experience should be planned. This is an area that can be a great problem if there is no method for evaluating students in the program. The more subjective the educational program and the less objective the evaluation of the students' performance, the greater the chance for a lawsuit. Although written records can be a nuisance, they are needed for legal protection.

Another concern with programs developed for longevity is that many of them start growing in size. It is quality not quantity we want, however, and the one should never be sacrificed for the other. Although athletic training educators and program directors are pressured to increase student enrollment, to perhaps save a sagging enrollment in the health/physical education department, or to provide other alternatives and options for employment, there are several factors that have to be considered:

1. Personnel—How much personnel do you have to control supervision of the program? I mentioned required written evaluations and the time involvement with educational records.

2. Facilities—You can only get so many people in a facility. That will depend upon the number and size of the facilities.

3. The size of the sports program—Three or four sports would not justify having 40 or 50 students.

Thus, the size of the program must be carefully kept within the limits of the guidelines established by the NATA.

The supervision aspect of the guidelines is very stringent and the limitation is six or eight students per clinical supervisor. That means qualified clinical supervisors and a certified athletic trainer is needed. Another limitation being investigated is the number of students allowed in a program. Even with 8 or 10 athletic trainers, with good facilities, an excellent program, and a major program with 30 sports for men and women, there may be a point where there is no return. Stringent limitations must be applied even with 8 or 10 trainers. Basically, we believe that the enrollment should be kept down and that there should be a formal written evaluation system for students.

It has been proven that curriculum revisitations that have had a formal program of clinical experience have done well. Their students have performed in the oral practical successfully, although this performance is only a trend and not statistically significant. Except for one or two programs, we find that the one-person educational program has lower scores on the certification exams. In a growing program with only one person, it is hard to see how that person can control and organize the program. It would seem that it is students who are educating other students. Especially with more than one facility, one person cannot be in all places at one time. He or she cannot be a classroom teacher, a clinical supervisor, and a program administrator, and still do justice to each and every student in a growing program. We do allow for one-person programs, but they must be kept within the boundaries of three or four students per one individual; one person, however, is not sufficient to operate a growing program. This does not mean that large programs do not have problems. The large programs must have communications between trainers about exactly what they are doing, teaching, and how they define students' responsibilities and evaluate their performance. So in either case, the program must be well planned.

Another problem is that most of our curriculum graduates are health and physical education majors, creating a vicious circle. The jobs are scarce in this area and greater in other teaching areas, although all education—teaching positions included—is being cut back. Nevertheless, we can place the English, music, or biology major sooner than the health and physical education major. The health and physical education majors, however, are the ones with the greatest interest: They are more intense in sports; they are more intense in the areas of anatomy, physiology, kinesiology, and training background. English majors, on the other hand, are less interested, have less background in sports, and may have to spend 5 or 5½ years in the program because the curriculum doesn't combine with their studies. So, we have more and more health and physical education majors wanting to enter the program while fewer and fewer jobs are available for them.

Because of this problem, we have to look at trends in schools around the nation in health and physical education with the nonteaching track option. The nonteaching track is trying to provide jobs for health and physical education majors besides the school setting. This is something we have to consider when we look at our guidelines because most of our guidelines definitely deal with having teaching credentials. There are many jobs as full-time trainers, or combination-type positions like working in the community as a trainer, related to fields like health and physical education, recreation, or health education, while serving as a trainer at the high school.

An extensive study of the curriculum graduates by Joanne Dolcemaschio for the Professional Education Committee demonstrated that approximately 50% attain athletic training positions upon graduation, 12 or 15% go on to graduate education, and the remainder are taking positions not in athletic training or are completely unemployed. This is because we are limiting people with the teacher-trainer credential when they decide to pursue teaching rather than training, or training and not teaching. Many of our people become employed at colleges rather than the high school level. One of the problems in any teaching field is that once students get to their senior year they want to teach high school. Then they realize the demands of a teacher-trainer and decide not to teach, at least not at the high school level. Some people drop completely out. They graduate from our curriculum, but do not want to be teacher-trainers. Although there are variables in this 50% employment rate, this percentage has stabilized for the last 3 or 4 years.

The Professional Education Committee encourages those with an excellent program to present it to the Committee. If the curriculum meets our guidelines, we can do nothing legally to keep that program from being evaluated. Remember, we are the only approval process for athletic training curricula. It may seem that we are playing the market when we continue to approve and acquire more and more curricula, yet at the same time, have a reapproval process to look at programs more and more stringently through the guidelines. We have changed our guidelines; we have revised them, and we are looking more toward quality education. In one year nine programs were placed on probation, meaning that those programs were required to formulate answers to their problem areas. These recommendations have to be completed within a year or loss of program approval results. I am not encouraging program development because the program must be good; it must be maintained within the guidelines. On the other hand, we must do a better job of promoting individuals for jobs, and I am talking about curricula. Although schools have no legal responsibility to go out and seek jobs for their students, this becomes more of a consideration when jobs are getting harder to get. This is something athletic training educators should think about. What can you do to promote jobs in your area? Can you help these people get jobs? Can you go out and sell in the field? You, as well as the national organization, should be selling. We cannot stop progress. We must keep moving forward.

Other areas of concern are rehabilitation and modalities. These areas must be taught by qualified experts in the field. We must evaluate how these courses are being taught and if they are being taught by someone qualified in the field. Another concern deals with the psychology requirement: Psychology is not enough for the athletic trainer; counselor education should also be considered because it provides actual methods for approaching individuals and athletes. This, too, needs consideration.

Another area of concern, besides evaluation of programs, is the screening selection and retention of students. This, like student evaluation, must be objective. Without objective criteria, you open yourself up for lawsuits. Again, this means more paperwork, but it is worth it.

What is the Professional Education Committee looking for in a program? One, any program must be based on the needs of the students and the needs of the geographical area. Programs should not be opened to create a job market; instead, they should be developed based on the need for trainers or teacher-trainers in a certain area. Another problem is that programs developed by the institutions and the administration want the trainer to take over the program. If this is not to your liking, you must stand up strong and explain how the apprenticeship program works.

Also, we would like programs to be as original as they can be. We are looking for the best type of educational program. We do not like to see programs that only meet the normal requirements. We want to see a program that is developed the best way for professionally preparing each student. If you are a true educator and interested in athletic training education, you will review the behavioral objectives, the skilled competencies, and develop your programs accordingly. For example, if one program has two courses in athletic training and requires 600 hours in clinical experience, you may decide that you cannot limit the program, that you have to have three or four courses and require more clinical experience. In this circumstance, you should use the ideas of many people instead of repeating ideas those one or two people developed earlier.

Also, the department housing your program should support it. This means released time and financial compensation should be given. If you are in athletics and getting paid 100% while actually doing 25% teaching, you should be given that compensation of 25% for teaching; you should not be expected to take on other jobs or duties and still have the same salary or a minimal increase of $50 or $100. The department should want a program, and if they want it to be a certain size, then they will have to provide enough personnel.

Next, there should be release time as compensation, not only for the program director but for supervisors of student trainers as well. Release time is common for other educational programs and athletic training education should not be slighted. In addition, the department must provide you with the proper equipment, supplies, and facilities. As the program director, clinical supervisor, or as an instructor, you should have the appropriate faculty status. You must have the faculty status so that you can operate the education program in your department, so you can attend the meetings, be a part of the meetings, and justify your program. You must be of an equal status when presenting your program and presenting revisions, and you must be able to represent your program yourself.

These are some of the things that we will be looking at when we review an educational program. I have not been trying to attack health and physical education departments because they have been the biggest help getting curricula started. When we initiated ideas about professional preparation for athletic training, we went to many different fields. We went to allied health fields, who could not recognize the value of athletic training, because at that time they were based in hospitals and this was not a hospital-based type of paramedical field. They could not understand what a trainer could do with the allied health relationship. So we approached the largest organization: HPER (which at that time was the American Association of Health, Physical Education, and Recreation), who gave us the help and support we needed. They recognized our professional preparation, guidelines, competencies, behavior objectives, and backed our programs in preparation. But today NATA wonders, are we housed in the right area? Should we be an allied health field? Should we be a department in itself?

AMA has recognized our efforts, has approached us and asked if they could assist us in accrediting our athletic training curricula. We did not accept at the time because we wanted to study all routes of becoming nationally recognized. We are not an accrediting agency; instead, we use an approval process or procedure, and there are tremendous differences between the two. We are trying to maintain the approval procedure until the time accreditation occurs. Currently, we have stricter requirements, and we can maintain stricter requirements on programs than through accreditation. Accreditation involves the entire institution rather than the program itself, so we must evaluate our status in the HPE area.

Examples of improvements in instructional areas could occur by offering better anatomy and physiology courses. Additional examples are cadaver anatomy, therapeutic modalities, and rehabilitation. If you have your own department, you must meet the health and physical education requirements, the university requirements, the department of education requirements, and then whatever is available becomes the athletic training curriculum, specialization, or option. If you are a department on your own, you develop your own program and then evaluate working with the department of education for a teaching credential. This allows greater strength than if you are aligned with another department. Developing an athletic training program or changing it does have problems. For example, if you don't maintain the size of the department you are not going to stay in existence. Do you want that many people now? Can you provide that many jobs if you have your own department? You must also make sure the program is truly a major and not just a glorified minor requiring two additional courses beyond the normal minor curriculum. What would be the difference between a major in athletic training and a program providing teacher-trainers?

The development of new courses is another area of concern: squeezing them in because of the requirements, trying to prepare for other teaching credentials, and adding hours on because of a limitation by the curricula—health, physical education, and other fields. You may be able to designate one institution that has several problems and is producing inferior graduates. You must review your shortcomings as a program director. The institution has to recognize the weak areas and give appropriate support, but it takes time to progress through committees. Although curricula producing graduates who fail the certification program must be re-evaluated, it must be remembered that change takes time; we as a committee have been establishing guidelines for only 10 years. There are no experts in predicting the future of athletic training.

Graduate education has some of the very same problems as undergraduate programs. Is the graduate program just a glorified undergraduate program? Is that the way we want it? Is it compensatory education for those in the field? Or should these programs be advanced educational programs building upon the base of an undergraduate program either through the curriculum or the apprenticeship route? Which way should it be? These are questions which must be answered if we are to point the way our graduate education should go. The high school faculty-trainer instructional programs were our first attempt to study alternative education methods. This attempt was experimental; these programs are not permanent, but temporary. It might be a better way of providing individuals for the teacher-trainer positions. We do not have any data to prove otherwise, as there are no certification results, nothing to justify negative reactions. I do not encourage the development of an experimental program because these undergo the toughest set of guidelines for approval that we have. The program must be developed with some consistency, but it has to be approved each year. If you advertise for students each year, you do not know from one year to the next if you are going to be able to have continued approval. This is why we only have two experimental programs which will continue to be evaluated.

We have other types of programs that vary from institution to institution. We have cooperative education programs—West Chester and Northeastern are two examples. Students complete off-campus clinicals, or students from other institutions receive the educational background from the approved institution. This is certainly a way of spreading responsibilities to different individuals and not creating impact on one school. Another option we are reviewing is to keep the committee abreast of the apprenticeship programs. We are reviewing plans to develop guidelines for institutions who want to try and improve their programs for apprenticeship. These guidelines will be totally optional, not mandatory.

This brings us back to continuing education to prevent obsolescence in the field of athletic training. Many different areas of sports medicine require us to increase our knowledge and skill. Remember that athletic trainers are educators who educate student athletes and student trainers about athletic training. They educate coaches—strength coaches, flexibility coaches, and even people who become educated about athletic medicine. We are even educating parents and physicians, helping to educate them about what we are doing in athletic training and what can be done. Remember, we, the Professional Education Committee, need the assistance of athletic trainers in providing answers to the questions that have been raised. We need input, regardless of whether it is new or revolutionary. We need new ideas. Remember, athletic training educators want the students they are supervising, regardless of the route they take, to be better prepared than themselves in the field. The only way this field is going to grow is if each and every person in the field is better than their teacher hoped and better than their teacher, at least better prepared. We can be considered educated athletic trainers only if we keep ourselves from becoming obsolete in the field by continuing our education.

Implementing a Clinical Experience
for Student Trainers

Rod Compton
East Carolina University

At East Carolina University (ECU), we have had basically the same clinical experience since 1970. We started an approved curriculum in 1975. The basic format remains the same as in 1977, when I presented information about our three-level clinical program. No major innovations have occurred since that time when the three different levels of student trainers were discussed in relation to achievement in the clinical aspect of the students' assignments. The academic assignments at ECU will not be discussed here, however.

We accept the students very young into our program, as young as we possibly can, and get them started early. One handicap in our program is that we do not have certified athletic trainers in nearby high schools for clinical experience. Therefore, we have chosen not to use this as an opportunity for the student trainers because the hours would not count toward NATA certification. All of their practical experience, therefore, goes into campus activities as trainers for athletic teams or physical education classes. The physical education classes are handled only for their immediate care problems. In athletics, our students will follow up, work closely with the athlete and the physician on an injury, and observe in the hospital and/or the doctor's office. The student trainers also become involved in the physical examinations with the physicians. We do not have an emergency room experience because the university has developed an involved medical school and allied health curriculum, including nursing and medical technology. These programs keep the emergency room schedule full.

In our program, we have three full-time certified athletic trainers, in-

Rod Compton MEd, ATC, is head athletic trainer at East Carolina University in Greenville, North Carolina.

cluding myself, and one or two graduate assistants are also available to take care of the intramurals. Again, it is with first aid care only; the students are not responsible for preventative-type programs or rehabilitation.

One tremendously beneficial aspect of our program is a preparticipation meeting every year before anything starts. We repeat a smaller type meeting at the middle of the year for anybody deciding halfway through the year that they want to start in sports medicine. Basically, this meeting is organizational, with standard activities such as filling out forms, meeting the administrators, and covering the policy and procedure manuals. We believe we have a unique situation, and in fact, we were among the first to do it. Our attorney gives a short talk on the legal obligations student trainers undertake and very seldom realize, and it is probably as a result of his talk that we normally lose two rookies per year at each meeting. Also, both we and our attorney strongly recommend liability insurance for participation in the program. We then have a question-and-answer session, where the veteran student trainers give the new students an idea of their experience or of situations that may arise. The student trainers are appreciative of this opportunity and relate well to the seniors.

Anyone who wants to go into sports medicine can, and at any level, but within the guidelines. For example, transfer students normally have not done well in our program. "Late bloomers" who decide their junior or senior year that they want to become trainers obviously have to spend additional time beyond their normal graduation schedule, but some of these people have become exceptional trainers. So, we have an open-ended policy, but have found that even though we have as many as 20 people at the initial meeting, by the time the first semester rolls around, that number is cut in half.

During the first year as a student trainer, clinical structure is open-ended and students can work as little or as much as they wish. Time requirements mean increased involvement their sophomore year, especially their junior year, and some in their senior year (other than when they are student teaching). But we do encourage students in their first year to try to spend most of their time in developing studies and grades. We have standard activities, for example, spending several hours on special taping techniques.

The most important things for students to accomplish in their first year are to observe our standard operating procedures and then to get to know the facilities and the personnel. Primarily, this encompasses the development of rapport between the trainers and the physicians and the relationship of the sports medicine team between the athletes and the coaches. But they do have the opportunity to help out, especially with routine duties, to the best of their abilities. Many rookies initially have a tendency to think they are more experienced than they actually are; they have to be reminded to work within their limits. We do have three certified trainers who keep the situation under control and do not put the rookies in decision-making situations.

Freshmen handle the laundry approximately once every 2 weeks and the washing of the whirlpools. We call this "sanitary engineering." We do even involve the rookies in game-type situations where they might be helping with hydratng (fluid replacement) or taking care of some of the athletes when the senior trainer, the certified trainer, or the team physician has recommended what should be done.

At the end of their rookie year (not necessarily their freshman year), all rookie trainers are evaluated by the full-time certified athletic trainers and by the team physician. At this point, an average of between two and five of these student trainers are put on the "student trainer staff." These students are the top 10 to 15 student trainers in our program. This selection is based on the student's performance during his/her rookie year or any additional years they may have had, an acceptable grade point average, and the ability to work with the student trainers and the other members of the staff. Those students not chosen for staff are not dropped from the program. In fact, they can remain in the curriculum and help out as much as possible, but they are assigned to help and assist the staff student trainers. The advantages of being a staff student trainer are receiving uniforms (practice and games), a $300-a-year stipend, and earlier athletic assignment. The athletic assignment allows progress toward becoming what we call a "charge trainer." We do not like to limit the responsibility of a charge trainer to a given academic level, a junior or a senior, for example, because some sophomores are mature enough to handle the charge trainer responsibilities. So we do not assign them by an academic rank. A "charge trainer" is responsible for the medical coverage of a nonrevenue sport.

Once we get into the courses, we require 15 hours of practical experience per week via our university policy. This guarantees a minimum of 150 hours per semester or more, although most of our students work far beyond this minimum. The only hours that we record are those supervised by a certified athletic trainer. Obviously, students put in many other additional hours, but we only count those hours that a certified trainer directly supervises.

We have two sports medicine practicum courses. These courses are very practical in nature. Students spend 2 hours a week in a seminar or lecture situation with me, one of our consultant lecturers, or one of our assistant trainers. We also cover CPR training during these 2 hours in different sessions. Unfortunately, we have only two true practicum courses. They are worth 3 semester hours each, so we can give them academic credit for some hours completed. We were limited to 6 credit hours for practical experience courses in the 4 years of schooling, so we made available three optional independent study courses. The first is worth 1 credit hour, the second is worth 2 credit hours, and the third is worth 3 credit hours. The students do the same thing as in the practicum courses but do not attend the 2-hour weekly seminar. They are graded on their activities and have to maintain a log book and other forms of recordkeeping. But, we have had very little interest in this nonstructured, "no-lecture-available-to-help-out-type" course, although it is available and it has been introduced to the students.

One valuable project in our course is called a "high school survey" program. The student trainers either select or are assigned a high school. They then are required to administer a 5-page survey form to this high school by getting answers and interviews with high school personnel and by observing what is happening at the high school. First, basic information on the school in general is recorded, such as enrollment classification, base salaries, sports offered, etc. Second, information is gathered on the trainer or person who handles the training duties at that high school. Third, basic information from the team physician or consultant is needed on what they cover and how they cover it, when they are available, and when they are not. Fourth, facilities, supplies, and budget are surveyed. Students have to make a line drawing of the facility in relation to the rest of the facility, and we also encourage them to take slides so that they can show their fellow student trainers. Fifth is insurance coverage: How does the high school handle their insurance coverage? Who is responsible in maintaining it? Sixth, they gather information on student trainers. The seventh area is general observations, and their evaluation is eighth. The students take this information and put it into an understandable format. It is filed and the file maintained because we later return to that same high school and repeat the same survey. Also, each student shares it in a seminar meeting with the other student trainers and they find out what problems may be encountered. The survey helps us because, at the college level, we become isolated with all our conveniences and appropriate materials. The students find out that high schools do not have luxuries like an electrical stimulator, ultrasound, four whirlpools, and so on. Our students have become shocked at the lack of facilities and salaries at the high school level. But the project has been well received and I encourage others to do it.

Another project we have is called a "rehabilitation project." We assign or the students choose an athlete with a particular problem and the students are responsible for rehabilitating this individual. They have to establish what the affliction is, its history, and then at what stage they took over rehabilitation. The rehabilitation program consists of using motivational techniques, exercise routines and devices, as well as recording measurements and writing up the project. When they are finished with the rehabilitation of the athlete or when the semester is over, they have to explain where they are in the program and explain the strengths or weaknesses of that particular rehabilitation activity. This project has received many compliments from former students.

Regarding participation, our first-year or rookie trainers spend an average of 6 or 8 hours per week in practical experience. Our curriculum trainers, those who did not make staff but continue in the program, average 8 to 10 hours per week. They are not in the course in which 15 hours are required. Staff student trainers average 15 to 22 hours per week throughout the year. The 4-year average (including those who drop out) for the curriculum student is 1,100 hours and 1,920 hours for staff student trainers. Some complete 2,500 to 2,600 hours or more over a 4-year period.

Our program is self-screening; we allow our trainers to make individualized paths and become deeply involved with the individuals. We do schedule females with football as well as with women's athletics. We also have the men work with women. In fact, when an individual comes in for treatment, anybody can work on anybody after consulting the athlete's file. The charge trainers, however, have priority.

Our student trainers also observe surgery; they even take care of prepping the individual or assisting in minor surgery. We have tremendous cooperation with our hospital. Our doctors encourage observation—not just orthopedic problems, but ear, nose, and throat problems, eye surgery, and others. We get involved and cooperate with our rescue squads with instruction in CPR training. We have excellent working relationships with our doctors and our student trainers leave the program feeling that they are personal friends with most of them.

We have a sports medicine conference offered once a year and have started using our senior student trainers and some of our staff student trainers to help instruct. It provides the staff student trainers with a great opportunity to become involved. This is a sophisticated sports medicine conference with something for all levels of experience, from the high school student trainers to the team physicians. We use physicians and certified athletic trainers as lecturers and lab situations for learning and practicing the basic skills. And finally, we have an open discussion at the end of the meeting about job opportunities. Our people leave with an honest evaluation of what is available at the high school level.

Our program is self-screening because of the number of hours available. Students can work as much as possible and cannot complain of lack of opportunities. We have deep involvement of all of our doctors who all teach a minimum of 2 hours a year or as much as 8 hours a year, in addition to working directly with the trainers on an injury. We do have three levels of achievement in addition to the regular standard grade rank, and these provide a healthy competition within a natural pecking order that makes things easier with administration of the program. We provide students with "hands on" experience from their first year on, coupled with a very strong classroom lab and lecture series in which the students almost immediately apply what they have learned.

The Student Trainer Clinical Experience at Lock Haven State College

David Tomasi
Lock Haven State College

The approach to clinical experiences in this paper is somewhat different than that discussed in the previous paper by Compton, although many of the same things are included. First, I bring in freshmen to observe what occurs in the training room. They acquire the name "gopher": they go for this, they go for that. By observing in the beginning, they find out what athletic training involves, and by mid-semester they have dropped considerably in number. By the second semester you find those students who truly want to be athletic trainers. The program is basically self-screening for the first 2 years; if students show interest, they remain.

Though the younger students may not know many of the concepts dealing with sport injuries, by the end of their sophomore year they have taken a course called "Safety Concepts," which certifies them as instructors in advanced first aid and CPR. This enables students to perform in emergency situations as well as those requiring first aid, and we use their ability to instruct as a reinforcing tool. By letting the students teach CPR from semester to semester, they keep up on all the current changes as well as reinforce their previous knowledge. I try to set them up with instructor jobs within the community so they learn to teach others than their peers. This experience enables students to call upon their knowledge quickly and accurately. From this course, they gain the ability to quickly evaluate not only sport-related injuries, but all injuries. Too many inaccurate evaluations are made at sights of accidents, especially those involving automobiles. Thus, placing a great deal of emphasis in this area will aid students in all types of future endeavors.

I also stress the importance of properly using equipment and of im-

David Tomasi, MS, ATC, is head athletic trainer at Lock Haven State College in Lock Haven, Pennsylvania.

provising in situations where the equipment necessary is not available. For example, we have been called upon the carpet because one of our students used a 35 MPH speed limit sign as a backboard. We believe that "If in doubt, splint the entire body." We teach the use of both the scoop stretcher and the backboard, because in a given situation you never know what type of equipment you are going to have. At Lock Haven State, we are fortunate to have everything we need but elsewhere our students may not be so lucky. Once the students know the equipment and how to use it, I make them practice and practice. I firmly believe that no one can practice too much.

Also included in the course outline is the proper sequence of the primary and secondary survey of an injury. This is of vital importance in evaluating any injury, because any error could be life-threatening. Once the student shows competence in this area we move to basic bandaging. Again, we put students in situations where they must work with limited supplies. We set up mock disasters in the town and have the students respond accordingly. In fact, one day I tied up the whole town for 5 hours. We had simulated a school bus accident requiring care of 32 people, and only three students knew it was a mock disaster. These are the kinds of experiences students must have in order to assure quick, accurate evaluations.

The other aspect of this course, CPR, is stressed greatly. The students must learn the proper use of oxygen and a suction device. I know most athletic situations do not have a suction device available, but I teach the whole gamut, because the American Red Cross certifies these individuals and expects this to be taught. Many other skills that relate only indirectly to athletic training may also have to be used in some situation. The hair traction splint is an excellent example of this. Few people know how to use this device even though it is very useful for locked knees; putting a little pressure on the splint may relieve the locked knee, and this device works as well as weights. All of these are important aspects of the total realm of first aid. Although we are protected by the Good Samaritan Act, we must still emphasize the importance of quick, accurate responses to any given situation, and students must have a broad, current knowledge of the techniques in order to make those responses.

The experience we try to give our students is the best possible clinical experience. As future instructors, they are taught so that when they become juniors and seniors they can turn around and teach the freshmen and sophomores. Not only do they teach them first aid but several athletic training procedures as well.

An important clinical experience that all my training students take part in is a working rapport with the hospital and staff, which we find to be very advantageous to our students. The student becomes a part of the emergency room staff, with liability coverage. The experience they get from working with the doctors and nurses can be experienced nowhere else. The students gain proficiency in taking the vital signs, blood pressure, heart rate, and respiration, although on most occasions these are checked by the nurse on duty. The students are made aware of ethics by the hospital administrator, whereas I serve as a consultant at these meetings.

Our success depends tremendously on our team physician, who is truly enthusiastic about sports medicine and helping our students in any way possible. Our physician is a chief surgeon at a hospital, and he makes time in his schedule to conduct a clinic for our athletes. Superb at relating information, he takes time out to explain everything to both the patient and the student trainers. He will usually try to be in the emergency room if one of our athletes requests him, which most do.

The radiologist at the hospital is also a big help to our students. He gives them a mini-course in the basic X-ray reading. Each student learns how to read the basics of an X-ray. All in all, the hospital experience is extremely worthwhile. Students gain experience in areas where in a normal training room situation they may not get the chance. By the end of their junior year, students have been exposed to just about everything involved in athletic training.

We have three training rooms to run and an operation staffed by only me, so the junior and senior trainers run those I am unable to handle. They know how to use the equipment in all the training rooms, and all the procedures are in written form and easily accessible. Again, the junior and senior trainers teach the younger students methods of using these modalities. I let the students make their own evaluation without my interjecting. In fact, I find they do better when I am not there watching them. They evaluate what they see alone, instead of depending upon my help. If they have any doubts or questions, they use me as a check.

Our students are also competent in setting up rehabilitation programs for athletes. We are fortunate to be one of the only schools of our size that has both a Cybex unit and an Orthotron. We stress the use of all equipment, most of which is up-to-date. We also spend a lot of time on simple things, such as how to use just a "hands on" technique. This is a vital skill, since many students may end up in a high school situation with little or no advanced equipment. I strongly stress rehabilitation, because this is such an important aspect of the training program.

The students are also required to take a physics course, which is a prerequisite to the use of physical modalities. The course is entitled "Physics for Health Science," but it is really physics for athletic training and gives the theory and the math necessary for all of the equipment used. This course is important to the student, who will be evaluated on physical modalities, on the indications and contraindications, and the physiology behind the use.

NAIRS (National Athletic Injury/Illness Reporting System) is something else students must learn. With NAIRS, each team trainer is responsible for the recording of injuries of their team. NAIRS is an excellent system and has assisted in lawsuits by providing complete information about the action taken by the athletic training staff on injuries. Lock Haven State gets a great deal of information from NAIRS, which is helpful to our program.

I have slides of many injuries that students may or may not see, which I show to the students often. We use these slides to point out injuries as they are actually seen at the time of the occurrence. The hospital is also helpful in sharing with us any interesting X-rays they may have.

The key to a good clinical experience is to allow the student trainer to handle as many problems as possible. The head trainer should act as a guide or the resource person, with the student administering the treatment to the injury. If I see the student is going to make a mistake, I will step in and say, "Think about it," and then allow him or her to continue. I believe that the best learning environment I can establish for my students is learning by experience. I allow the juniors and the seniors in the program to make most of the decisions with my supervision. After all, the head trainer knows enough to not need the practice, but the student needs both the practice and the reinforcement.

Developing Objective Criteria
for Evaluating Student Athletic Trainers

Linda Treadway
Central Michigan University

Defining objectives for evaluating student athletic trainers is a difficult area; we are still searching for a good method at Central Michigan University (CMU). It is significantly easier to give students a written test and grade an answer sheet than evaluate what happens in the clinical situation. At CMU, we list the ideas and suggestions that we know and value. The evaluative tool, because it covers so many observed areas, has become long and complicated. Therefore, the first thing one should do is to set up objectives that the evaluative tool should reflect. A copy of these objectives should be given to the students so that they know what is expected of them.

Our clinical experience comes after a basic introductory course and the students' first practical exposure in the training room. Unlike the remainder of their clinical time, the first two semesters of clinical exposure are graded for credit. After the students become established as trainers and are assigned to teams, we still evaluate them on different skills and relationships, interpersonal relationships, and professional conduct, but do not give them a grade. We have two types of evaluation: graded and nongraded. The initial two semesters that the students are in the training room, they are not assigned to a team and therefore do not develop a relationship with the coach. They do work with the team physician, however, but not as extensively as the staff student trainers, who are assigned to specific sports.

The first practical course has a list of objectives. At the initial class meeting, we give the students the list of objectives and indicate what we

Linda Treadway, MS, ATC, is former athletic trainer at Central Michigan University in Mount Pleasant and currently a certified athletic trainer for Stunts Unlimited in Westminster, California.

expect them to accomplish before the end of the semester. This provides a solid basis for evaluation and prevents repercussions at the end of the semester, because students are initially told what is expected of them. The more aggressive students ask questions and push themselves to learn, whereas other students must be prodded and encouraged to become more involved.

Another problem area is the organization of time; this encompasses the semester, quarter, or year in which the objectives must be accomplished. We structure the practicum at CMU to avoid the problem of students missing objectives. Specifically, we have organized some of the skills, knowledge, and background theory for athletic training by covering a different skill each week in the class meeting and expecting the students to practice and perfect those skills throughout the week. Thus, if we are busy or out of town, the students still have a competency to develop. Because the faculty trainers are often busy and cannot spend as much time as they would like with each student, our veteran student trainers help out tremendously. Once the rookies or practicum students have the initial exposure to the skills, they can practice them with the input of the third and fourth-year student trainers. In this way, the students perfect the skills that are tested and examined during the semester. This procedure motivates students to make strides in their practicum and enables them to learn something each week.

The practicum includes a scavenger hunt to aid in one of our initial objectives which is to learn the location of everything in the training room. In addition, we hold a reverse scavenger hunt in which students must quickly return 30 items to their correct place. Both of these activities are fun learning experiences and are just two examples of the creative things that can be done in an athletic training program.

I feel guilty if I do not teach something every day, so in the two major training rooms, I put up a ''fact for the day'' for review by the students. These cover such things as anatomy, emergency care, and rehabilitation. They also stimulate questions and discussions in the training room. Organization is important and prevents students in the clinical experience from just putting in time.

Finally, I tell my students to hang around me like vultures, because it is much easier to learn while I am evaluating an injured athlete. It is easier for me to explain something if someone is standing right beside me than if I have to drag someone over to observe. If students are not on the spot, I usually complete my job without them.

The instructor should evaluate the students several times during the year, and the evaluation form should reflect the objectives that were developed from the start. At CMU, some of these are the physical skills that NATA requires. We hand out a copy of the certification competency list of skills to all the students, and when applying for the certification exam, they submit this list with each skill initialed and dated. This method assures that the students complete all the required skills. As stated earlier, these skills must be reviewed so the students know the objectives they have to meet and the criteria used to evaluate them. These evaluations can be completed regularly and kept in their files.

Instructors must also devise an evaluation form for their own particular situation, because schools have different designs with different skill requirements. It is a good idea to organize the whole educational experience for the student trainer and develop objectives for each year. A checklist is a good format for evaluation.

When constructing a checklist or evaluation form, organize the objectives and behavioral responses into categories, such as prevention of injury, first aid, emergency care, treatment, rehabilitation, and taping and wrapping. Think of all the important aspects that comprise a trainer. It is also important to have records and evaluations of the student's personal conduct and professional development. Frankly, athletic training is not just knowing how to tape, but knowing how to relate to the students, team physicians, coaches, and trainers. All of this should be included in the evaluation. An important area of the evaluative tool is the definition of your grading technique; for example, A through E, 1 through 5, or excellent, good, very good, poor, needs elaboration or definition. Otherwise, the students will bicker over numbers. Quantitatively defining grades will limit such problems. For example, write out the number system as it applies to skills or personality traits. Be sure to leave room for written comments and to elaborate specifically on an evaluation, because it is more meaningful for both you and the students. Finally, the students should evaluate your clinical experience and in fact your whole program. Their feedback will improve the program, especially because the strengths and weaknesses of a program change constantly. The once-a-week meeting in our practicum course was partly initiated by student comments, for example.

I doubt if anyone has a perfect way of evaluating a clinical situation. I know we do not, but we are constantly trying to strive for better ways to evaluate. The main thing is to set objectives that reflect your evaluative tool and to definitely allow feedback from your students in order to critique your weaknesses and your strengths.

Evaluating Student Clinical Performance

Danny T. Foster
University of Iowa

The University of Iowa has operated a NATA-approved athletic training education program for the past 5 years. During these 5 years, we have continually improved our background in constructing educational objectives and in evaluating their outcomes. The objectives of the student athletic trainer's clinical experience are aimed at the application of principles and concepts to a wide variety of situations in order to provide depth to clinical experience. In this paper, I will discuss the procedures taken to develop instruments used at Iowa for the evaluation of student clinical performance.

Our view of educational measurements in the clinical setting has depended strongly on the concepts of validity and reliability. We wanted a method of measuring student achievement that produced specific information. This procedure allowed us to identify a simple and logical method that should produce valid results. In this same context, we looked for an instrument that was free of bias, to give every student an equal opportunity to perform the behaviors that we purposely observed and an instrument that would be consistent with the formal instruction students received prior to performance in the clinical setting. From experience, we at the University of Iowa agree that the behaviors observed and evaluated are critical to successful professional practice.

We also looked for a method of evaluation that would consistently provide stable and trustworthy estimates of observed behavior. We can compare clinical reliability to essay scores reported by two or more competent readers. When two or more judges of clinical experience are used, the reliability of the evaluations can be directly estimated and expressed as a correlation-type index. If only one judge is used, however, then the

Danny Foster, MS, ATC, is an athletic trainer at the University of Iowa in Iowa City.

reliability of the evaluations must be made on a logical basis. The decisions about clinical settings or evaluation instruments which result in better agreement among competent clinical instructors generally are likely to improve the reliability of the clinical evaluations.

We also looked closely at our clinical setting before arriving at some guidelines that helped develop our clinical evaluation instruments. The clinical setting at the University of Iowa usually offers a one-to-one interaction primarily between the student and the athlete. This type of interaction clearly eliminates standardized evaluation procedures for groups and simultaneously combines student attitudes and values with their thinking processes. Measurement of student achievement can be derived from real-life situations, because students interact individually with athletes, coaches, and physicians in various settings and because they perform relevant activities in the clinic or in a simulated setting.

Who observes the students? As a Big Ten school, we had to consider the balance between the time required to observe a performance and the time available to watch that performance. We believe that observations in the clinical setting are most valid if they are personally and purposely observed. Unfortunately, our supervisors normally have only limited time available for student observation; therefore, the options open were to use short forms for the evaluation or to have more people observing specific aspects of clinical experience in order to obtain a composite view of the student's performance. The clinical supervisors assisted in the development of the evaluation forms and participated in individual training sessions on evaluation procedures.

Where are observations made? We have continually confronted the problem that if observations are made in the training room, then the evaluation of the student's performance may be secondary to the primary goal of service to the athlete. Likewise, if an instructor intervenes to correct faulty procedures, then the final product cannot be taken as an accurate sample of the student's achievement. Of course, the advantage of observing student performance is that it is reality; therefore, there should be maximum transfer of learning from the clinical setting to a professional position in athletic training. Other problems involved with the training room experience include the following: (a) an inability to standardize the patient base; (b) a difficulty in comparing students because, as students see different athletes, they have no equivalent or standard set of problems; and (c) considerable variation in the rate of athlete contact, so that some students may see twice as many athletic injuries as others. Obviously, the disadvantages of the real-life settings are the advantages of simulated settings (i.e., learning and evaluation are now the primary goals, and these settings may be instituted where student errors may be "costly" or when it is not possible to make real-life observations). Another strategy associated with problem solving in the clinical setting may be to review clinical cases prepared by the student. These cases require that the student design a plan of treatment or critically analyze previous treatment plans. These case plans can be reviewed whenever time allows, but they do not allow for observation of interpersonal contact nor for the actual enactment of care.

What behaviors are important? The observations of student behaviors reflect three types of learning outcomes important to clinical education: cognitive, psychomotor, and affective. Whenever it is not essential to view actual application of knowledge, we use written evaluation instruments to answer cognitive problems. Psychomotor outcomes are arranged observations that involve motor skills in the student's interaction with athletes. Not only athletes but also coaches and physicians respond to the personal traits of the students as much or more than to the cognitive or psychomotor skills. These affective outcomes, however, present many problems in measurement. Because numerous possible explanations exist for any single student behavior, many behaviors must be observed before inferring the presence or absence of a personal characteristic.

Our objectives and considerations about the evaluation of student clinical experience set the groundrules for the guidelines in developing our clinical evaluation instruments. At Iowa, we use three types of instruments: rating scales, checklists, and anecdotal records. Rating scales are used when a clinical supervisor evaluates student performance on scaled behavior or numerical categories. These scales cover broad ranges of student characteristics and permit judgments about the quality or quantity of the behavior being observed. The scales seem most appropriate for global-type observations of a small number of characteristics. When using a series of items that describe student behaviors, a checklist is most appropriate. These lists are concerned primarily with presence or absence of certain behaviors, not with quality. We have used checklists to tally minimum competency behaviors. Anecdotal records ask the observer to describe positive or negative events. These descriptions allow specific focus to be placed on satisfactory or deficient areas.

We believe that our evaluation instruments are valid and that the outcomes of the evaluation are important and reliable. Clear instructions provide us with a common base for all raters to improve reliability. The forms allow an economical use of time and energy and can stand on their own; thus, they are likely to be used and used accurately. Each form contains a preface of clear instructions explaining use of the form, explanation of potentially ambiguous terms, description of the setting, and use of the results.

We use items that evaluate stable characteristics which are critical to successful performance and which reflect intended instructional outcomes. Key factors in the development of these forms were observer comments obtained on former students in which common positive and negative traits were noted. Meetings were arranged among the staff members to identify the behaviors that were characteristic of professional athletic trainers. These characteristics were clearly defined in order to produce reliable evaluations. We were very conscious of the general notion of "goodness" and "badness" which might influence the ratings, and therefore, we organized objective criteria to increase validity, thereby decreasing the "halo-effect." Some of the raters always marked in the middle of the scale or used a "straight ticket" because they believed that criticism may hamper student motivation or lead to insecurity in performance. We were not overconcerned about this behavior but have worked and will continue to work at resolving the conflicts associated with an attitude of learning from mistakes. We have found that evaluations are most appropriate and remembered when performed on the spot or with a minimum of time delay from observation to reporting.

Finally, we suggest that scoring of the instrument be related to the use of the information, which should reflect the minimum level of competency to which the athlete is entitled. Every student who graduates from our program has to meet this standard as a basic requirement.

Evaluating Student Athletic Trainers with Objective Criteria

Skip Vosler
Ohio University

At Ohio University, evaluation of each student is performed on what we call the "4-year" plan. The students are required to have 2,400 hours of clinical experience, which is broken down into 600 hours for the freshmen and 1,800 hours for the upperclassmen. The upperclassmen, along with my assistants and myself, help evaluate the freshmen. The evaluation of the upperclassmen is completed by the senior student trainers, my assistants, and me. We found that evaluating students only once a year is not adequate, so we decided to evaluate the student trainers each quarter.

Students came into the office to discuss any problem areas and then evaluated themselves. It was amazing to find out how highly they regarded themselves. One of the problems that we discovered in using the yearly evaluation tool was that the students did not clearly understand their role within the curriculum and the clinical experience. They believed that they were doing all that they needed to do, and therefore gave themselves a higher ranking. The quarterly evaluation enabled the student trainers' clinical experience to be more compatible with my own expectations.

We tried several things with this mechanism; one was the appraisal of the student trainers' progress. We are continuing to develop our appraisal mechanism, reviewing it each quarter. We use the old form for the upperclassmen and the new form for the freshmen. This evaluation tool helps us make changes within the clinical experience by enabling us to discuss with the students why they were low or high in a certain area. Thus, we can change the curriculum to better meet the students' needs.

The student must elaborate about all areas of the clinical experience on

Skip Vosler, MS, ATC, is head athletic trainer at Ohio University in Athens, Ohio.

this form, which creates one problem encountered with any type of evaluation form; that is, it can be either too short or too long. The evaluation tool at Ohio University is too long because it includes all areas of the clinical experience and therefore areas in which some students might not be working. For example, the freshmen would not be involved in rehabilitation, conditioning, or working with coaches. Thus, the freshmen use only part of the form, whereas the upperclassmen fill it out entirely. Although the form is long, we decided that it was nevertheless the best way to cover all the areas of the curriculum.

We found that a numerical scoring system of 1 through 10—breaking the scores into such numbers as 8.5, 6.3, and so on—did not work because neither the students nor I understood it. Therefore, we have changed our system to a scale line from 1 through 5, adding NA for "non-applicable." The taping technique and treatment technique areas, as well as rehabilitation, conditioning, and the clinical experience, receive grades of A, B, or C. The seniors and juniors working with the coaches in their particular sport are graded in the actual situation. We only grade them this way because how a student reacts and handles a situation cannot be accurately evaluated in a false setting. And although professional growth is hard to measure, our team physician—who spends a lot of time with the students—helps perform this evaluation.

The coaches' viewpoint is also included in the student-trainer evaluation. At Ohio University, we try to make the coach realize that a student trainer is as responsible for the program as I am if I were there. Although the coaches' contribution is important, to make sure that they don't evaluate students only negatively, I personally discuss each student with the coach and perform the evaluation with him or her. I have found that the coach is more fair this way.

It is very important for students to be responsible during all 4 years, but at the same time, it is not important for them to receive a grade. We have eliminated grades for the clinical experience, and the Health and Physical Education Curriculum Committees have agreed with this.We now require the students to have 2,400 hours to be able to graduate from the curriculum, and they are not approved until they complete this requirement. Our evaluation tool is not perfect, but then I do not know what a perfect evaluation tool is.

The Need for Subjectivity and Objectivity in the Athletic Training Evaluation

Gerald W. Bell
University of Illinois

In 1968, B.S. Bloom wrote that "if the evaluation system informs the student of his making of a subject, he should develop greater confidence in his ability and will subsequently be encouraged to continue learning." In this article, Bloom alluded to the relationship between academic performance, mental health, and self-concept, in that "since a student's ego development is affected by the evaluations his [trainer] preceptor makes of him, his confidence and ability to perform can be reinforced by rewarding experiences" (Note 1, p. 62).

Because of the importance of the evaluation to students' learning, performance, and self-concept, the evaluation must be encompassing and informative. It must include the three behavioral objectives of cognitive, affective, and psychomotor skills required in athletic training. Athletic training deals with cognitive skills in its theoretical area and affective skills in the interactions with coaches, athletic trainers, athletes, and team physicians; finally, it involves daily athletic training room techniques of injury evaluation and injury management through treatments and preventative strapping and preventative instruction programs. An evaluation that excludes any of these areas certainly cannot help, and may hinder, the student athletic trainer's performance and progress.

A good evaluation requires that instructors develop objectives for successful performance in the classroom, in the field, and in the clinic. Krathwohl (1964, pp. 178-179) stated that an evaluation should determine students' attainment of the following objectives: "Acquiescence in responding [compliance], willingness to respond [accepts responsibility] and satisfaction in response [enjoyment of self expression]." He also

Gerald W. Bell, EdD, RPT, ATC, is NATA curriculum director at the University of Illinois in Urbana-Champaign.

believed that students must show a "sensitivity to human need."

Mager (1962) believed that the preparation of instructional objectives should first include a statement of instructional objectives, that is, a collection of words or symbols describing one of the instructor's educational intents. This objective should describe exactly what students must perform to demonstrate achievement in the course and the criteria by which the instructor ascertains that the students are performing what they should. Third, in describing terminal behavior, or what the student must do, the instructor must identify and name the overall behavior, define the important conditions under which the behavior is to occur (given restrictions and limitations), and define the criteria of acceptable performance. Finally, the instructor should write a separate statement for each objective; the more statements an instructor writes, the better chance he or she has of making clear the educational intent of the course.

Evaluation, then, refers to judging performance as specified by acceptable criteria and as determined by the evaluator, in this case, athletic trainers. Bloom (1956, p. 207) stated that evaluation is a judgment about the value of material for given purposes. Involved in this evaluation are quantitative and qualitative judgments about the extent to which material and methods satisfy criteria as well as the use of a standard appraisal. He further stated that instructors evaluate their students by two kinds of judgments—internal evidence (logic) and external evidence (remembered). Also, as Stufflebeam (1971) pointed out, the administrators must take part in maintaining a high level of evaluation, for only with high standards can the status of the athletic training profession be increased.

The general procedures instructors should use for measuring and evaluating, as outlined by Burton (1962, p. 33), are as follows:

1. Determine what is to be measured.

2. Define objectives in pupil behavior (student trainers).

3. Select or design an instrument-situations appropriate for measuring the outcome.

4. Record results.

5. Evaluate evidence and make judgments.

6. Ensure that evaluations are continuous and participatory.

7. Follow up with diagnosis.

Burton asserted that the evaluation of the pupil is an evaluation of the teacher as well.

Bloom (1971, pp. 193-194), like Burton, believed that evaluation creates improvement of both teaching and learning. He believed that of paramount importance in an evaluation is a "system of quality control in which it may be determined at each step in the teaching and learning process whether the process is effective or not, and what changes must be made to ensure the effectiveness of the process before it is too late." He recommended that evaluation be a synthesis of the learning process or "the putting together of elements and parts so as to form a whole . . . with divergent thinking . . . where the student provides a unique response and the evaluator determines the merit of the response."

A constructive, positive evaluation experience is a mechanism that can help students develop confidence in themselves. As stated earlier, a positive evaluation must be encompassing; it must include both objective and subjective aspects. Although the instructor must set down criteria for determining an evaluation, as Burton (1962, p. 166) stated "the learning experience should be broad" and "should provide opportunity for success in meeting needs and solving problems through . . . a natural integration of feeling-doing-thinking." Thus, a broad learning experience, which should include achievement of both objective and subjective skills, should be judged by an evaluation of the same scope.

Students must know what is expected of them, and they might meet several skill abilities; however, they may still be unable to perform as athletic trainers. Human performance requires task analysis—that is, evaluation—to provide better information in order to make decisions. The behavioral objectives must be stated in terminal, observable behavior and described in the conditions under which the behavior should occur and with specified criteria of acceptable performance that can be quantifiably measured on an evaluation. A combination of a subjective and objective evaluation, along with student involvement and knowledge of expectations, is vital in developing the thinking athletic trainer.

Reference Note

1. Bloom, B.S. *Learning for mastery: Evaluation comment I.* Los Angeles: Center for Study of Evaluation of Instruction Programs, May 1968.

References

BLOOM, B.S. (Ed.). *Taxonomy of educational objectives: The classification of goals. Handbook I: Cognitive domain.* New York: Longmass, Green, & Co., 1956.

BLOOM, B.S., Hastings, J.T., & Medaus, G.P. *Handbook of formative and summaritive evaluation of student learning.* New York: McGraw-Hill, 1971.

BURTON, W.H. *The guidance of learning activities.* New York: Appleton-Century-Crofts, 1962.

KRATHWOHL, D.R. (Ed.). *Taxonomy of educational objectives and curriculum of educational goals. Handbook II: Affective domain.* New York: David McKay, 1964.

MAGER, R.F. *Preparing instructional objectives.* Palo Alto, CA: Fearon, 1962.

STUFFLEBEAM, D.L., Foley, W.J., Gephart, W.J., Guba, E.G., Hammond, R.I., Merriman, H.O., & Provus, M.M. *Educational evaluations and decision making.* Bloomington, IN: Phi Delta Kappa, 1971.

Instructional Improvement
in the College Classroom

Lawrence M. Aleamoni
University of Arizona

Instruction comprises an instructor, a textbook, a television presentation or a film presentation. What is taught in the classroom may vary from excellent to poor, applicable to useless, and understood to misunderstood. What is *learned*, however, is not necessarily what is taught. Therefore, to determine the extent, type, and degree of learning in a classroom, some method of evaluation is necessary.

Almost every instructor seeks information on the effectiveness of their instruction. For certain instructors, such information will be used to evaluate the performance of their students. For others, it will be used to evaluate their own performance and possibly the appropriateness of the course materials, organization, instructional method, and so on.

If instruction is to be effective some interaction must exist between what the instructor presents and what the students comprehend. Therefore, the instructor needs information on one major aspect of the instructor-student interaction: knowledge of student learning. This knowledge should be provided to (a) the students, so that they may be constantly aware of their progress in comparison to others in the class and in comparison to course standards, and (b) the instructor, so that s/he may alter the instructional rate, content, or method in order to suit the desired learning.

If instructors wish to evaluate their instructional effectiveness, they must first determine what should be evaluated. For example, instructors wishing to determine how much subject matter their students have learned in a given course will typically examine those students at the end

Lawrence Aleamoni, PhD, is director of the Office of Instructional Research and Development and professor of educational psychology at the University of Arizona in Tucson, Arizona.

of the course. In doing so, they are assuming that all of the students entered the course with a specified (definable) level of knowledge about the subject matter, which is generally not the case. Obtaining accurate information about the modification and expansion of students' knowledge as well as when in the instructional flow this may or may not have occurred can be extremely valuable in trying to improve one's instructional effectiveness.

Instructional effectiveness can be evaluated with a series of sequential activities that are a direct result of an instructor's decision to teach (Aleamoni, Note 1). The experienced and successful instructor will usually do the following:

1. Decide upon the goals (general instructional objectives) and level of student performance desired at the end of the instruction;

2. Select subject matter, materials, and the teaching methods relevant to the objectives and performance desired;

3. Cause the students to interact with the appropriate subject matter in accordance with principles of learning and motivation; and

4. Measure and evaluate the students' performance according to the objectives and/or goals originally selected.

Testing

Probably the most common means of obtaining data for evaluating changes in one's students is the test or examination. Tests or examinations are generally considered to be indicators (or gauges) providing both the instructor and the student information about the degree to which both have been successful in achieving the instructional objectives. This means, therefore, that unless the objectives are clearly defined for both the instructor and students, and unless the tests measure performance in terms of the objectives, the tests will at best be misleading; at worst they will be irrelevant, unfair, or useless (Aleamoni, Note 1). Unless instructors have a clear picture of their instructional intent, they will be unable to select (or construct) test items that clearly reflect their students' ability to perform the desired skills or that reflect how well students can demonstrate their acquisition of desired information.

Students generally study and learn the material that is tested, not necessarily the material that is presented. Tests used in a course represent, in a very practical manner, the direction an instructor thinks the students should go; this, in turn, determines the emphasis that the students will place on the material covered. Good tests can therefore orient student efforts into relevant learning activities, while the development of the tests and the knowledge of student responses can help the instructor improve the instruction (Aleamoni, 1971).

Every instructor who has constructed an examination realizes how difficult this task is. Not only must the examination provide an adequate sample of the objectives of the course, but it must also be reliable, valid, practical, and useful. No single type of examination is best suited to measure certain aspects of learning. Rather, the quality of a test depends on the instructor's mastery of the knowledge to be tested and his or her experience with that type of examination (Aleamoni, Note 2).

Evaluation and Grading

Once the instructor constructs a high quality examination, then his or her next responsibility is to accurately evaluate the results of the examination and report the level and quality of student learning. College instructors are usually required to evaluate other forms of student work in addition to examinations (Brown & Thornton, 1971). For example, they must judge and rate oral reports, term papers, book reports, class participation, or the performance of certain manipulative skills. The following questions suggest a general approach to evaluate such measurements (Brown & Thornton, 1971):

1. What criteria are available or needed to rate or judge such student work?

2. What are the major elements of the process or product in which excellence may be demonstrated?

3. What are the significant subelements of the process or product with which the total rating must be concerned?

4. What is the relative importance (or weight) of each?

5. What are the bases for scaling performances or products?

6. What will be the range of scaling (e.g., from "excellent" to "satisfactory")?

7. What criteria will be used to determine the range limits of each rating on the continuum?

8. If a final overall rating is needed, how will it be determined?

9. Will this overall rating be the average of the weighted ratings of all elements combined?

10. How will it be reported to the students?

Students should be provided with all of the above criterion information so that they can use them as aids in preparing the products and performances on which they will be judged. This also would allow them to assess the strengths and weaknesses of their efforts.

The instructor's evaluation of student performance on tests and other assignments or tasks are typically translated into letter grades. These grades are used as a basis for evaluating student achievement rather than as a means of describing such evaluation because they are considered (a) an appropriate means of providing feedback to the student about how s/he is progressing, (b) to be a fairly reliable and valid index of academic achievement, (c) to have common interpretations, thereby allowing the interchange of relatively standardized information about students between schools, (d) as a means of motivating the students to learn, and (e) as a basis of sorting and certifying students for numerous administrative purposes both within and outside the institution (Pascal & Geis, Note 3).

Grades are judgments that reflect a set of complex and sometimes irrelevant and subjective variables such as attendance, sex, neatness, and so forth. What goes into a grade varies from one instructor to another, as shown by the widely differing distribution of grades by instructors of multisection courses who have the same standards of achievement (Ericksen & Bluestone, Note 4). The methods instructors use in assigning grades may provide some insight into why grading is so difficult.

Although course grades are sometimes still based exclusively on a single end-of-course examination, by far the more common practice is to combine the grades students earn in several different course activities (e.g., term papers, book reports, oral reports, discussion, quizzes, midterms, and finals). To determine each student's final grade, the instructor generally performs the following tasks: (a) assesses and grades the student's performance in each of the several different activities, (b) assigns suitable weights to each separate grade, and (c) combines the separate grades into a single grade in a manner that recognizes their varying weights, their variability, and the practices of the institution (Brown & Thornton, 1971).

Instructors typically resort to either "grading on the curve" or "percent grading" in order to rate the student's performance in each of the several different course activities.

Grading on the Curve

With this method, instructors use normal curve characteristics to determine the percentage of the group to be assigned each grade in order to indicate a student's achievement relative to that of his/her peers. One technique of grading on the curve is to assume that the students' performance in the classroom will be distributed like a normal curve, so that there should be 3% As, 13% Bs, 68% Cs, 13% Ds, and 3% Fs. Another technique entails using the mean and standard deviation of the actual distribution of student classroom performance and specifying that students with scores more than 1.5 standard deviations above the class mean will receive As, those between .5 and 1.5 standard deviations above the class mean will receive Bs, and so on (Ebel, 1965). The major difference between these two techniques is that the first one predetermines the percentage of students receiving each grade, whereas the second one does not.

Grading on a curve has both advantages and disadvantages. Some of its advantages are that they allegedly help prepare students for the competition of life because scores on a curve are themselves competitive. Also, grades motivate students to work and learn, and they are a fairly reliable and valid index of academic achievement.

The disadvantages of grading on a curve slightly outweigh the advantages, however. The percentages used in such grading are arbitrary, and different groups can be expected to depart from such preconceived distributions. Also, the grades are not standardized; they do not tell anyone—either the student, the instructor, or the employer—specifically what the student has actually learned or not learned. And finally, grades as rewards may promote grade-getting behavior.

Percent Grading Method

Instructors using this method define a student's achievement according to some absolute standard by identifying in advance percentage score ranges that will be associated with each grade. For example, a student with a score in the 90 to 100 percent range would qualify for a grade of A, and so on.

The alleged benefits of percent grading are similar to those of grading on the curve. In addition, it clearly relates achievement to degree of mastery of what was set out to be learned, and it provides fixed, standard measures of achievement so that the students do not compete against each other (Ebel, 1965).

Unfortunately, percent grading often fails to live up to its promise of providing truly meaningful and stable measures of achievement. Some of its alleged defects are that performance standards are typically based on instructor observations of what students typically can do. This means that the standards are more relative than absolute. Also, if no one falls in the highest score range, does it indicate a problem with the teaching, student learning, or grading system?

An Alternate Grading Method

A grading system cannot be all things to all people. A single symbol cannot represent low achievement from one point of view (i.e., actual degree of subject matter mastery) and high achievement from another (i.e., progress in relation to reasonable expectation). What it can and should have is one clearly defined and scrupulously guarded kind of meaning. College and department faculties have the opportunity and the obligation to establish and maintain clearly defined meanings for the symbols used in their grading systems.

Grades should represent the degree of achievement in the course. This implies an adequate sampling of subject matter on a competitive basis by means of tests or other valid appraisals. Describing student qualities, characteristics, or achievements in terms of various letter grades might be done somewhat as follows (Brown & Thornton, 1971):

A — Signifies that both major and minor instructional objectives have been achieved and the work is of superior quality; reserved for outstanding students who are clearly capable of going on to do advanced work in the field.

B — Major instructional objectives achieved with excellent, above average, standards; some minor objectives not achieved; students easily capable of doing the next stage of advanced work in the field.

C — Major instructional objectives achieved with minimum acceptability; many minor objectives not achieved; work of average quality; students minimally capable of doing advanced work in the field, with no major handicaps to performance.

D — Most major objectives not achieved with even limited acceptability; below average work, but above failure.

E — No major objectives achieved; work of unacceptable quality.

This is substantially more informative than the typical definition of grades, which can be found in the latest University of Arizona General Catalog (1979):

A — Excellent
B — Good
C — Fair
D — Poor
E — Failure

The following points should be considered in order to reduce the difficulty encountered in grading (Aleamoni, 1979):

1. The grading system should put the students in competition with well-defined standards of excellence, rather than with each other.

2. The instructor can and should determine at the beginning of a course what s/he expects the students to know and do after completing the course.

3. The instructor should predetermine the percent of material on which students must demonstrate mastery for particular grades.

4. Grades ought to reflect how well students have acquired the knowledge they committed themselves to study.

5. Test scores or project scores should not be converted to letter grades before combining them to determine the final grade. Such a procedure results in the loss of information. One should convert all scores to standard scores (e.g., T-scores), then weight and sum them. Grades should then be assigned to the summed and weighted standard score distribution.

6. Do not use the natural breaks in score distributions as justification for assigning different grades, because such breaks are due to chance alone.

Instructors may need to gather and refine their evaluation information for at least 1 year before implementing a system that accurately reflects the quantity and quality of student learning according to instructor and course expectations. This means that the standards used to arrive at grades should be carefully gauged to the instructional expectations of student performance.

Conclusions

It should be apparent that if instructors take the necessary steps to (a) clearly define what is expected of the students, (b) inform the students of these expectations, (c) select and organize the subject matter, materials, and teaching methods to accomplish those expectations, (d) develop valid and reliable measures of student performance, and (e) develop an accurate and meaningful grading system, then both instructors and their students will be more satisfied with the instructional efforts. A poorly organized course, irrelevant examinations, and grade inflation are symptoms of instructors not following these steps.

Reference Notes

1. Aleamoni, L.M. Developing instructional objectives (Note to the faculty, No. 4). Office of Instructional Research and Development, University of Arizona, Tucson, AZ, 1977.
2. Aleamoni, L.M. Kinds of examinations (Technical Report No. 1). Measurement and Research Division, Office of Instructional Resources, University of Illinois, Champaign, IL, 1968.
3. Pascal, C.E., & Geis, G.I. An outline of methods of grading student performance (*Learning and Development*, 5[5]). Centre for Learning and Development, McGill University, Montreal, Quebec, Canada, 1974.
4. Ericksen, S.C., & Bluestone, B.Z. Grading ≠ evaluation (Memo to the faculty, No. 46). Center for Research on Learning and Teaching, University of Michigan, Ann Arbor, MI, 1971.

References

ALEAMONI, L.M. MERMAC: A model and system for instructional test and questionnaire analysis. *Behavioral Research Methods and Instrumentation*, 1971, 3, 213-216.

ALEAMONI, L.M. Why is grading difficult? *National Association of Colleges and Teachers of Agriculture Journal*, 1979, 23, 7-8.

BROWN, J.W., & Thornton, J.W., Jr. *College teaching: A systematic approach* (2nd ed.). New York: McGraw-Hill, 1971.

EBEL, R.L. *Measuring educational achievement.* New Jersey: Prentice-Hall, 1965.

Methods for Successfully Teaching Student Athletic Trainers

Richard F. Irvin
Oregon State University

When teaching students how to manage injuries, athletic trainers should consider both their teaching technique and their technique in injury management. This paper is most concerned with the teaching aspect.

Typically, athletic trainers arrive at a teaching situation from a background of a clinical rather than an extensive teaching experience. For this reason, most athletic trainers should make an effort to evaluate their teaching methods and techniques.

All athletic trainers do some teaching, which can occur in a variety of situations. These situations might include teaching an athlete a rehabilitation routine; teaching a group of athletes a preventative procedure; teaching one or more athletic training students in a practicum or internship situation; teaching a formal theory athletic training class; or teaching a workshop, clinic, or seminar.

Trainers working with athlete-patients should be especially concerned with their teaching. Management of injuries is most successful when athletes participate in and become involved with their own treatment. Also, for legal reasons, athletes must know the necessary details of the proposed treatment. By informing athletes of the therapeutic aspects of their own treatment, athletic trainers are demonstrating legal responsibility.

Becoming an effective teacher takes some planning. In preparing a lesson or lecture, athletic trainers should take into account the following: (a) the selection and organization of the content; (b) the selection of the presentation method; (c) the instructional resources; (d) the conditions for successful learning; and (e) evaluation of teacher effectiveness.

Richard Irvin, PhD, RPT, ATC, is NATA curriculum director at Oregon State University in Corvallis, Oregon.

Selecting and Organizing the Content

Athletic training is a problem-solving profession, so prospective athletic trainers must be taught to *think* as well as to learn basic facts; that is, they must learn how to apply the facts and principles they have learned in class in a variety of practical and theoretical environments. The material, then, should be organized along the same lines that the practicing athletic trainer would use in the clinical situation:

facts ──▶ concepts ──▶ principles ──▶ other applications

When selecting and organizing course content, the athletic teacher-trainer should first formulate the course or behavioral objectives he or she wishes to achieve. This gives the presentation breadth and depth. Next, the instructor should develop a topical outline. For instance, in a course on the upper extremity, the outline would cover each landmark in that structure—for example, the acromioclavicular joint, the sterno-clavicular joint, the shoulder girdle, etc. This topical outline not only outlines the structure itself, but establishes the organization of the course as well.

The instructor should then construct a detailed outline of the subjects s/he wishes to cover in relation to the upper extremity. This outline would cover such things as function anatomy, prevention of injury, including the fitting and maintenance of protective equipment, skill technique, conditioning, and warm-up. These subjects would be followed by the discussion of the mechanism of injury, athletic first aid, evaluation, treatment, and rehabilitation of an injury to the upper extremity.

Finally, the instructor should consider the acquisition and utilization of information. What resources are available to the students? How much of their time should be spent in the classroom and how much in the clinical setting? This last objective—the utilization of information—leads back to the first; that is, teaching the students to think, to analyze the facts learned in the classroom and apply them in the field.

Selecting the Method of Presentation

The method of presentation should encompass an instructor's most effective teaching personality, the existing conditions and resources available, and the behavioral objectives or desired outcomes of the course. The educational research literature would be invaluable reading to athletic teacher-trainers.

There are two basic approaches to presenting a lecture: informal or formal. Shown in Table 1 are the advantages of the formal and the informal teaching technique.

Table 1

Formal Teaching Technique	Informal Teaching Technique
More material can be covered.	Allows for student questions or comments.
Instructor can maintain continuity and flow of ideas.	Offers an active reaction to the presentation.
Instructor can maintain a planned schedule.	Provides for adequate feedback as to whether students are comprehending.

Choosing Instructional Resources

Instructors can employ a variety of instructional resources to enhance a course. They can ask guest speakers to come in and lecture about a particular aspect of the subject matter. Graphic materials, audio recordings, slides, and films or videotapes all can help students learn the material more easily while at the same time make the learning a more enjoyable and varied experience. When choosing from among such resources, instructors must take into account those which will best motivate the students, those which will most assist students in acquiring the knowledge, and those which will help students to use the knowledge in the future.

Conditions for Successful Learning

Along with providing various instructional resources for lecture presentation, athletic teacher-trainers must prepare the students for each lecture or lesson. In addition to reading assignments, instructors can provide their students with various materials to not only prepare them for the lecture but for examinations as well. Vocabulary lists, main concept handouts, and study guides can all help facilitate student learning.

Evaluation of Teaching Effectiveness

Examinations partially indicate how students are progressing in a course, and they also are useful for evaluating teacher effectiveness. Written examinations can be in either objective or essay form. The objective test measures students' mastery of facts and concepts, whereas essays evaluate students' ability to organize the concepts or express their own opinion. A practical examination will measure students' functional performance. A combination of these three types of examinations may provide the best measure of students' achievement in a course.

Students also should be given an opportunity to participate in evaluating the teaching process. The teacher evaluation should include at a minimum a rating of the instructor's mastery of the subject matter, the organization of the course, the clarity of the presentation, and finally, the overall effectiveness of the course.

A Proposed Athletic Training Curriculum Design

Sue Halstead
University of Virginia

The role of the athletic trainer has, in the past, been the responsibility of personnel ranging from the student manager to the coach in Virginia's high schools. In the future, it is hoped that qualified, trained, and certificated athletic trainers would perform the duties of injury prevention, treatment, and rehabilitation. Through the Division of Continuing Education, the staff of the Physical Education Department at the University of Virginia has designed an athletic training curriculum that would be implemented for the training of high school coaches and teachers already employed within the Virginia public school system. Coaches, physical education teachers, and teachers with strong science backgrounds will be the target population for education and professional training.

The following curricular design is a 1½-year, 21-hour credit program, designed from the current National Athletic Training Association (NATA)-approved graduate athletic training curriculum of the University of Virginia's School of Education. This NATA-approved curriculum is currently the only one in the Commonwealth of Virginia (see Table 1).

Course Descriptions

EDHP 525: Athletic Injuries—3 Hours

The course work includes a basic study of human physiology and anatomy relevant to different athletic activities. Such conditions as stress, long and short duration events, and acclimation are addressed. The basic anatomical and physiological differences between male and

Sue Halstead, MEd, ATC, is an assistant athletic trainer at the University of Virginia in Charlottesville, Virginia.

47

Table 1

NATA-Approved Curriculum for the Virginia Commonwealth

EDHP 525	Athletic Injuries (3) Taught on Location—Semester 1, Year 1
EDHP 582	The Art & Science of Sports Medicine (3) Taught at University of Virginia—1 week, summer
EDHP 793	Emergency Medical Technician Taught on Location—Semester 2, Year 1
EDHP 739	Practicum in Athletic Training (3, 3) Taught on Location back to back during Semester 2, Year 1, and Semester 1, Year 2
EDHP 720	Advanced Athletic Training (3) Taught on Location—Semester 1, Year 1
EDHP 583	Sport Psychology Seminar (3) Taught at University of Virginia—1 week, summer

Shown in Table 2 is an illustration of how such a program may be implemented:

Table 2

Timetable for Athletic Training Program

	Fall	Spring	Summer	Fall
1979	EDHP 525			
1980		EDHP 739 EDHP 793	EDHP 582 EDHP 583	EDHP 720 EDHP 739

female athletes, as well as physical training implications of these differences, are emphasized. Course work also emphasizes competencies, knowledge, and experiences in the area of athletic training. This includes a basic understanding of the medical and physiological implications of athletic training as well as the principles, procedures, and techniques in the prevention, treatment, and rehabilitation of athletic training.

EDHP 582: The Art and Science of Sports Medicine—3 Hours

This is a 1-week course seminar in athletic training. It concentrates on prevention, evaluation, treatment, and rehabilitation of athletic injuries. Speakers in the course include physicians, athletic trainers, and physiologists from a variety of sport backgrounds.

EDHP 793: Emergency Medical Technician—3 Hours

The emergency medical technician course trains individuals in the management of accidental and medical emergencies. The application of skills required in this course results in reduction of patient morbidity and mortality, as well as in the alleviation of pain and suffering. A broad spectrum of topics is discussed, including the appropriate emergency management of coronary artery disease, cardiac arrest, fractures, shock, thermal injuries, emergency childbirth, and emergency medical conditions. Successful completion of this course will result in EMT certification by the Commonwealth of Virginia, State Department of Health, and CPR certification by the American Heart Association.

EDHP 739: Practicum in Athletic Training—6 Hours

This course is a clinical and practical experience, enabling students to work with athletes in the treatment and rehabilitation of athletic injuries; it also emphasizes the establishment of rapport with coaches and team physicians. A certified NATA trainer observes and supervises the record keeping, organizing, and administering of training room routine.

EDHP 720: Advanced Athletic Training—3 Hours

This course assists the student in diagnosing, treating, and rehabilitating orthopedic injuries particular to athletes. These skills include application of therapeutic modalities, as well as the development of rehabilitation and condition regimens. Students will also become familiar with administrative techniques, which include serving as a liaison between parents, athletes, coaches, school administration, athletic director, team physician, orthopedic surgeon, family practitioner, and dentist.

EDHP 583: Sport Psychology Seminar—3 Hours

This seminar is a 1-week concentrated course presenting individual lectures on topics pertaining to sport psychology. Topics of particular interest include self-psyching for improved performance, motivational techniques in sports, personality and the successful athlete, psychosocial influences in athletics, planning and practicing for maximum performance, and athletics for special populations. Student participation and sports skills are emphasized to reflect athletic competition stress and anxiety.

PART TWO

ATHLETIC INJURIES

Anatomy and Selected Biomechanical Aspects of the Shoulder

James S. Keene
University of Wisconsin

Anatomy can be a very dry topic, but like a good dry martini, if the anatomical ingredients are blended into a palatable presentation, it can be both interesting and informative. This paper, then, will focus on the anatomy and functions of the shoulder that are relevant to the evaluation and treatment of athletic injuries.

To look at the shoulder "up close and personal," it is necessary to discuss the complex shoulder mechanism in terms of its four basic components. These components include the: (a) super structure—bony components, (b) moving parts—joints involved, (c) motor power—musculature, and (d) communications network—brachial plexus.

The super structure of the shoulder is comprised of three bones: the clavicle, scapula, and humerus. The clavicle is a superficial S-shaped bone that acts as a "boom" from which the upper extremity is suspended. This S-shape gives the clavicle great resilience. The clavicle also provides the only bony connection between the shoulder girdle and the thorax through the sternoclavicular joint. Because it is the only bone of the shoulder girdle that articulates with the thorax, it acts as a shock absorber for the entire upper extremity. When an individual lands on the hand, the force is transmitted through the shoulder to the clavicle and onto the sternoclavicular joint. The clavicle also protects the brachial plexus beneath it.

The architecture and muscle attachments of the clavicle explain the great vulnerability of this bone to injury. The lateral portion is flattened and lacks a medullary cavity. Progressing medially, the bone becomes triangular, and at the junction of the lateral and medial portions (the

James Keene, MD, is an orthopedist and team physician at the University of Wisconsin in Madison, Wisconsin.

middle third), the clavicle is only covered by fascia and skin. At this point, the bone is subcutaneous and unprotected. In addition, the middle third is also the site of the change in the S-curve and the configuration of the bone and therefore is the most common site of clavicular fracture. Because of its form and function, the clavicle is the most frequently fractured bone in the body.

The scapula is the second bone of the superstructure. This bone is flat, triangular in shape, and translucent; it has a soft contour and a posterior location over ribs 2 through 7. The upper eight ribs form the track over which the scapula swings. The only intervening structures between the scapula and the ribs are the subscapularis and the intercostal muscles. Most of the weight of the scapula is contained in several prominences and rugged processes located near the glenohumeral joint.

The scapula's function is mainly that of muscle attachment. It is essentially suspended on the thorax by the muscles attached to it. The important anterior anatomical landmarks include the blade (body), the neck of the scapula, the coracoid process, and the subscapular fossa. On the dorsal surface, we find the supraspinatus and infraspinatus fossae separated by the spine of the scapula. The spine continues laterally to form the large acromion process. Inferior to the acromion process is the glenoid cavity, which will be reviewed in greater detail shortly. Viewed from above, the normal tilt of the glenoid is 2 to $-12°$. Abnormal angulation of the glenoid in relation to the rest of the scapula is thought to be a cause of recurrent shoulder dislocation. In several cases of recurrent dislocation, excessive anteversion of up to $25°$ has been documented.

Comparative anatomy may help you remember some of the important prominences and the shape of the scapula. The upper extremity of an upright individual allows extremes of motion. In humans, the shoulder has the greatest motion as a joint complex of any in the body. Four-legged animals do not need a free-swinging shoulder and therefore do not have a large infraspinatus fossa or infraspinatus muscle, nor do they need a large acromion process to protect the head of their humerus. Due to changes in the requirements of the muscles and the function of the shoulder in humans, however, both the infraspinatus fossa and the acromion process are greatly enlarged. These bony changes address the importance of the muscles originating at these sites. The infraspinatus muscle has a much greater role in humans for stabilizing the humerus, and the deltoid muscle, which attaches to the acromion process, is much larger in humans; the increased size of the acromion indicates the deltoid's more dominant role.

The third bony component of the super structure is the humerus. This bone is equal to 1/5 of the body's height and its landmarks are the head, the neck, and the shaft. Because the scapula in humans has rotated to a more posterior position than found in four-legged animals, the head of the humerus also changed. In humans, the head of the humerus rotated in a posterior direction and therefore assumed a retroverted position. This retroversion averages 16°. The head also forms an angle with the humeral neck of about 135°. The important bony prominences in athletic injuries are the tuberosities of the humerus: the greater tuberosity and the lesser tuberosity. Between these tuberosities lies the bicipital groove, through which the long head of the biceps muscle moves. During abduction of the arm, the greater tuberosity can impinge on the acromion. This is very important to consider in throwing, swimming, and other overhand sports, because the impingement can cause wear and tear on the rotator cuff muscles, which attach to the greater tuberosity.

Fractures of the humerus occur either at the surgical or anatomical neck. The surgical neck is appropriately named, for this is where most fractures occur. Because the surgical neck is the thinnest part of the neck of the humerus, it is the most vulnerable area for fracture. The anatomical neck is where the capsule from the glenoid attaches to the humeral head. The deltoid tubercle is the attachment of the deltoid muscles to the humerus. In humans, this tubercle has migrated distally, thus giving the deltoid a greater mechanical advantage for the important functions of abducting and flexing the arm. Because of the human's erect posture, the scapula has rotated dorsally so that elbow motion can occur in an anterior-posterior plane. This scapular rotation and subsequent humeral retroversion has resulted in the more medial position of the greater and lesser tuberosities and biceps groove. Thus, the course of the biceps tendon has been changed and is therefore more vulnerable to injury. This appears to be one of the disadvantages of upright posture and a free-swinging upper extremity.

In summary, then, the basic landmarks of the super structure are as follows. The clavicle is subcutaneous and palpable throughout its length. The acromion process is the most superior projection of the scapula and is palpable through the skin. The greater tuberosity is the most lateral prominence of the shoulder. The coracoid process can be felt one to two finger breadths below the clavicle through the anterior deltoid fibers, and the acromioclavicular joint is felt as a shallow depression between the outer portion of the clavicle and the acromion. And finally, the bicipital groove is located anteriomedially below the acromion, where one can palpate the long head of the biceps.

Next, what are the "moving parts" of the shoulder? The term shoulder joint is misleading because this joint includes no less than four independent articulations: the sternoclavicular joint, the acromioclavicular joint, the scapulothoracic joint, and the glenohumeral joint. Although each joint is a separate entity and capable of independent motion, all of them contribute to the total motion of the shoulder joint. An extremely important fact is that motion in these four joints is simultaneous and *not* successive. Shoulder joint motion is a result of the synchronous participation of four joints.

The first of the four joints is the sternoclavicular joint. In general, this joint has the greatest inherent stability of any joint in the body, and it has the function, if not the form, of a ball and socket-type joint. This great inherent stability is due to the strong costoclavicular ligaments holding the clavicle down to the rib and the sternoclavicular and interclavicular ligaments that hold the clavicle to the sternum and attach it to the opposite clavicle. This joint also has an articular disc and a synovial lining. The sternoclavicular joint can be injured, although only infrequently, because of its strong ligaments and bony configuration.

Scapulothoracic joint motion occurs between the anterior aspect of the scapula and the thorax. The scapulothoracic joint is formed by muscles suspending the scapula on the rib cage and the intervening subscapularis and intercostal muscles. The scapulothoracic joint has a great deal of mobility and allows us to whip the upper extremity.

The third joint, which is more well known, is the acromioclavicular joint. This joint has an intra-articular disc and the configuration of a gliding joint. It is stabilized by several ligaments. The superior acromioclavicular ligament is mechanically inefficient in preventing upward displacement of the clavicle, but is efficient in preventing anterior and posterior displacement. The key to stability of the AC joint is the suspensory ligaments of the upper extremities: the conoid and trapezoid ligaments. These ligaments are named for their shape. The conically shaped conoid ligament is the most medial and anterior ligament; it goes from the coracoid process to the clavicle. The rectangular trapezoid ligament also travels from the coracoid process to the clavicle, but has a more posterior and lateral position than the conoid ligament. The third ligament is the coracoacromial ligament, which runs between the two prominences for which it is named. The most important stabilizers of the acromioclavicular joint are the conoid and trapezoid ligaments, however.

The fourth joint of the shoulder is the glenohumeral joint, a ball-and-socket joint. The socket (the glenoid) is only ⅓ the size of the ball (the humeral head), however, thus making it fairly unstable. This anatomical arrangement permits the glenohumeral joint the greatest range of motion of any joint in the body, but its increased motion means decreased stability. Therefore, it is the most frequently dislocated large joint in the body.

Changes in the shape of the humeral head can also lead to recurrent dislocation. You may get a compression fracture in the hemispherical head with first dislocations as the head moves in an anterior direction on the glenoid. This alteration of the head, called a Hill-Sach's lesion, is one of the essential lesions in recurrent dislocations and in failures of repairs of recurrent dislocations. The ligaments of the glenohumeral joint are found in the capsule and are thickenings or extensions of the capsule. There are three such ligaments—the superior, middle, and inferior—although they are not identifiable in everyone. These ligaments, which originate from the glenoid, are palpable at surgery, and each one is approximately 4 millimeters thick and about a centimeter wide. The superior ligament attaches to the lesser tuberosity, the middle ligament attaches below the insertion of the subscapularis, and the inferior ligament goes from the origin of the triceps to the surgical neck of the humerus. These ligaments have openings between them, and one area that is thought to be the site of anterior dislocation is the opening between the middle and inferior glenohumeral ligaments. Other ligaments, such as the coracohumeral ligament, function to hold the humerus in the glenoid. The transverse ligament holds the biceps tendon in its groove.

The joint capsule is attached to the glenoid through the glenoid labrum. The labrum is a thickened, fibrocartilaginous part of the capsule that attaches to the glenoid and, in conjunction with the bony glenoid, increases the size of the socket. When the labrum becomes detached, it does not necessarily heal back to the glenoid properly; therefore, some investigators feel that a detached glenoid labrum is the "essential lesion" in recurrent anterior shoulder dislocations.

In summary, the lesions that cause persistent instability in the shoulder include: (a) the Hill-Sach's lesion, which is the defect or a compression fracture in the posterior-lateral aspect of the humeral head; (b) a torn glenoid labrum; (c) laxity or tears in the joint capsule; and (d) excessive anteversion of the glenoid.

Now, putting the joints together, we can examine how they work simultaneously and synchronously. First, shoulder motion must be described in several planes. The terms used are forward flexion, lateral flexion or abduction, inward and outward rotation, horizontal abduction-adduction, and circumduction. The motions together provide a certain, unchangeable scapulohumeral rhythm. The humerus moves in relation to the scapula with a constant ratio between the two bones. Shoulder motion can be divided into two phases of motion, the first is the setting phase. The setting phase occurs in the first 60° of forward flexion and the first 30° of abduction. During this phase, the scapula seeks its most stable position on the chest wall. This motion differs between individuals; in some people the scapula just "vibrates." After the setting phase, there seems to be a fairly fixed 2:1 ratio of glenohumeral to scapulothoracic motion; that is, for every 15° of glenohumeral motion, there is 10° of scapulothoracic motion.

When determining glenohumeral motion, the scapula must be held and the motion measured as the patient abducts his or her arm. The individual with a fused glenohumeral joint may demonstrate 120° of abduction, but this is due to scapulothoracic motion, not glenohumeral motion. It is best to record shoulder motion at the scapulothoracic and glenohumeral joints separately. This can only be done by palpating the scapula.

Clavicular motion also plays an important role in shoulder movement. The continuous rotation of the scapula at the scapulothoracic joint depends on clavicular motion. There is a total of 60° of elevation and 50° of rotation of the clavicle. During glenohumeral and scapulothoracic motion, 40° of elevation occurs at the sternoclavicular joint (in a 10:4 ratio). During the first 30° and after 135° of abduction, a total of 20° of elevation occurs at the acromioclavicular joint. To get full scapulothoracic motion and full abduction of the arm, the clavicle must rotate. Researchers have verified this rotation by placing pins in the clavicle of volunteers and observing pin motion from the side as the individual abducted the arm. Rotation of the clavicle averaged 50°, and all these individuals had normal acromioclavicular and coracoclavicular ligaments. Therefore, as the arm is abducted, these ligaments must elongate and allow the clavicle to rotate on its horizontal axis.

The third component of the shoulder mechanism is the musculature that acts on these joints. Instead of examining the innervations or individual functions of each muscle, the muscles will be reviewed by topographical and functional groups. The muscles that originate from the scapula and insert on the humerus (scapulohumeral group) are the deltoid, subscapularis, teres major, supraspinatus, infraspinatus, and teres minor. The deltoid in humans—an upright animal—constitutes 41% of all the shoulder musculature and is a massive and multipennate muscle. In unipennate muscles, the fibers originate at one tendon, traverse the length of the muscle, and end at the tendon of insertion. In the deltoid or the multipennate muscles, many of the fibers do not go the length of the muscle and reinsert in the muscle septa. This gives multipennate muscles great power and mechanical advantage for their short excursion. An important part of the deltoid muscle that is often surgically or athletically injured is the anterior fibers originating off the clavicle. Damaging these may limit forward flexion of the arm. Many surgical approaches recently have been modified as the importance of these anterior fibers has been realized.

The function of the deltoid is mainly forward flexion and abduction of the arm. The deltoid cannot initiate abduction, however; it starts working after the supraspinatus muscle (rotator cuff) initiates abduction. Individuals who have paralysis of the rotator cuff must dip their shoulder to give the deltoid a better mechanical advantage so that it can initiate abduction of the arm.

Related to the deltoid is the subdeltoid and subacromial bursa. A bursa is best defined as a little fluid pillow that sits between a muscle or tendon and any bony prominence. This fluid pillow is not filled with much fluid unless it becomes irritated or inflamed. Inflammation happens in athletes and middle-aged individuals with repetitive and overuse syndromes in the shoulder. The subcoracoid bursa and a subscapular bursa also can become inflamed.

The rotator cuff is a group of four scapulohumeral muscles. These are the "SIT" muscles and the subscapularis muscle. The SIT muscles are the supraspinatus, infraspinatus, and teres minor, and they all insert along the greater tuberosity and cover the superior and posterior aspects of the humeral head. These muscles are the external rotators of the shoulder and are prone to injury when the arm is abducted because of their attachment to the greater tuberosity. Vascular studies indicate that there is an avascular area that may tear with repetitive abduction due to impingement of the cuff muscles between the greater tuberosity and the acromion. The SIT muscles are the three superior and posterior muscles of the rotator cuff. The subscapularis muscle originates in the subscapular fossa and inserts on the lesser tuberosity of the humerus. It is one of the major adductors of the arm and one of the primary medial rotators. It also holds the humeral head against the glenoid for the deltoid and the supraspinatus to act on.

The axial-scapular muscles—the trapezius, rhomboids, serratus anterior, and levator scapulae—are muscles that originate on the trunk and insert on the scapula. They function as a group to stabilize the scapular base and allow the upper extremity to be whipped about without subsequent winging of the scapula. The trapezius is a large, thin muscle with a broad origin from the spines of C1 to T12 and inserts on the clavicle and the spine of the scapula. The serratus anterior originates from the medial border of the scapula and inserts along the anterior ribs. This muscle prevents winging of the scapula. The trapezius and serratus anterior hold the scapula against the chest wall. The rhomboids, located underneath the trapezius along the medial aspect of the scapula, hold the scapula in its retracted position. The levator scapulae originates from the cervical spine and inserts on the spine of the scapula. Its sole function is elevation of the scapula.

The third topographical group of muscles is the axiohumeral group, which originates on the trunk and inserts on the humerus. The muscles in this group are the pectoralis major, pectoralis minor, and latissimus dorsi. The pectoralis major originates from the medial third of the sternum, the clavicle, and ribs 2-6, and it inserts on the crest of the greater tuberosity of the humerus. The latissimus dorsi has a broad origin from the spinous processes of T6-T12 and the lumbosacral fascia and inserts between the teres major and the pectoralis major. It functions as one of the extensors and internal rotators of the humerus. A good way to remember the insertion of these muscles is to remember the saying, "a lady between two majors,'' the lady being the latissimus dorsi, and the two majors the pectoralis major and the teres major.

The upper arm musculature does not fit into any of the previous groups. These important muscles are the triceps with its three heads (the long head traversing to an intraglenoid insertion), and the biceps with two heads, one to the coracoid process and one traversing the bicipital groove to the supraglenoid tubercle. The biceps flexes the elbow only when the forearm is supinated. If you pronate your forearm and flex the elbow, as in front rowing, the biceps is flaccid. The biceps will supinate the forearm only when the elbow is extended.

The last component of the shoulder mechanism examined here is the communications network: the brachial plexus. The brachial plexus is composed of roots, trunks, divisions, cords, and branches. Another mnemonic helpful in remembering these components is ''Robert Taylor Drinks Cold Beer.'' The brachial plexus emerges between the anterior scalene and the middle scalene muscles. It is then protected by the clavicle as it runs under the cover of musculature into the upper extremity. The plexus originates as the ventral rami or roots C5, 6, 7, 8, and T1. The long thoracic nerve which innervates the serratus anterior originates from these ventral rami. With an avulsion of the plexus, the loss of the long thoracic nerves will cause winging of the scapula. The phrenic nerve is another nerve at this level, but the long thoracic is the most important nerve in this paper. The dorsal scapula nerve also originates from these roots and innervates the rhomboids and levator scapulae. Primarily, however, the brachial plexus originates from the ventral rami of roots C5-C8 and T1.

The five roots of the plexus form three trunks: a superior, middle, and inferior trunk. The C5 and 6 roots form the superior trunk, the C7 root forms the middle trunk, and the C8 and T1 roots form the lower trunk. Brachial plexus stretch injuries or ''burners'' occur at the upper trunk. All three trunks divide to form anterior and posterior divisions. Those nerves that originate from the anterior divisions go to the muscles on the volar or anterior side of the arm, and the nerves originating from the posterior divisions go to the muscles located on the posterior aspect of the arm. Next, the brachial plexus divides into lateral, posterior, and medial cords. The cords are named according to their relationship with the subclavian artery. The lateral cord is lateral to the artery, the posterior cord is behind the artery, and the medial cord is medial to the artery.

The brachial plexus terminates in five branches: the musculocutaneous, median, ulnar, radial, and axillary nerves. The axillary nerve innervates the teres minor, and the deltoid; the radial nerve innervates the triceps and the posterior muscles of the forearm; and the anterior branches, which are the ulnar, musculocutaneous, and median nerves, innervate the anterior muscles of the arm and forearm.

In summary, then, the shoulder is a functional unit of three bones, four joints, three topographical muscle groups, and the brachial plexus. Its motion is due to synchronous, simultaneous participation of all joints and muscles. More specifically, the glenohumeral joint has the greatest motion but the least stability of all the large joints in the body. Finally, although the brachial plexus is the shoulder's well-protected nerve network, it is vulnerable to injury.

Shoulder Problems in Athletes

William G. Clancy, Jr.
University of Wisconsin

Brachial Plexus Injuries

Brachial plexus injuries can and do occur in contact sports. Frequently these injuries are considered minor; they often go unrecognized, receiving minimal treatment. A spectrum of brachial plexus injuries is seen in contact sports. The most common and fortunately the least severe is that of a transitory stretch of the brachial plexus, which produces a burning pain radiating from the neck down the arm, often extending into the hand. This injury may also produce numbness and tingling after the burning pain has subsided. In addition, there is weakness of the upper extremity due to both the pain and the transitory paresis, which is the result of the stretch of the nerve fibers in the plexus. The athlete is unable to use the involved extremity until the pain and weakness has subsided, which usually takes only a minute or two. This injury is often referred to as a "burner or a cervical nerve pinch." Because this injury frequently abates within a few minutes, allowing the athlete to return to participation, many pay little attention to it, missing the more serious brachial plexus injuries.

To better understand these injuries, it is important to review the anatomy of the brachial plexus (see Figure 1). The nerve fibers from the nerve roots of C5, C6, C7, and C8, together with some contributions from C4 and T1, unite to form three trunks, namely the upper, middle and lower. The nerve fibers in these trunks subsequently divide to form three more structures, the lateral, medial, and posterior cords, from which the fibers emerge to form the peripheral nerves.

William Clancy, MD, is an orthopedist at the University of Wisconsin in Madison, Wisconsin.

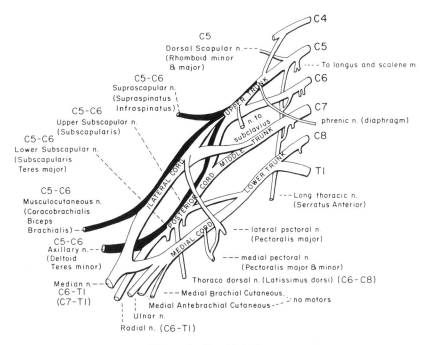

Figure 1—Brachial plexus.

Proximally, the plexus is fixed to the spinal cord and by fibrous tissue in the vertebral foramina, and distally to the muscle fibers. If the neck is turned or flexed away from the plexus and the shoulder is driven downward or backward, tension is developed in the plexus. If the load is high, significant stretch is placed upon the plexus and injury to the plexus can occur. The injury severity ranges from a very mild stretch within the physiologic limits of the nerve fibers, producing the so-called burner, to complete avulsion of the nerve root or trunk, resulting in severe paralysis.

Classification of Brachial Plexus Injury

To classify these injuries, we must understand that each nerve trunk is composed of thousands and thousands of individual nerve fibers and that there may be a spectrum of injury to the many nerve fibers within the trunk. If a single nerve fiber has been stretched within its physiologic limits and without any structural damage resulting in an interruption of its ability to carry an electrical impulse, the injury is called a neurapraxia. This interruption is transitory. If the stretch is of greater magnitude, some nerve fibers or axons, which are the tail of the motor neuron in the spinal cord, undergo complete degeneration. This nerve injury is called axontomesis. The muscle fibers innervated by the injured axon will no longer contract.

Because there are thousands of nerve fibers within the plexus and there is usually a spectrum of injury, it is impossible to classify these injuries based on a single nerve fiber injury. I have therefore devised a classification of plexus injuries based on the clinical and electromyographic evaluation. This classification is a summation of the various injuries within the plexus and allows one to determine when an athlete may resume competition.

A grade I injury means that there has been only a transitory loss of function, with full recovery usually occurring within minutes, but in some cases up to 2 weeks. Motor testing of all the muscles about the shoulder and arm are equal in strength, power, and endurance to the opposite side. Electromyography at 2 weeks would not demonstrate any loss of motor units or fibrillations.

A grade II injury would result in some mild but clinically detectable weakness which has not fully recovered within 2 weeks. Although there is reasonably good strength, some weakness is still present. Electromyography at 2 weeks will show signs of axon degeneration. This consists of decreased motor units and the presence of fibrillation potentials.

A grade III injury consists of the clinical finding of gross weakness about the shoulder and arm which has not recovered within a year. Again, there will be positive electromyographical findings, and in rare cases, a pseudomeningocele indicating a root avulsion.

Prognosis and Return to Competition

A grade I injury consists of a stretch of the plexus within its physiologic limits without any effect on muscle function. Some axons may have sustained permanent injury but are too few to be picked up on EMG and to affect muscle function. Competition can be resumed on complete return of function and strength.

A mild grade II injury means that some slight weakness persists for more than 2 weeks; it is a result of a significant number of axons being injured. Return to competition is allowed whenever there is full return of strength, power, and endurance. The time of functional recovery varies from 3 weeks to 3 months. In a severe grade II injury, it may take 6 months to a year for full recovery.

A grade III injury means that although there is still some muscle function, there has been a severe injury to the plexus, with destruction of a great number of axons. Because regeneration occurs at a rate of approximately 1mm a day, it will take approximately 6 months to a year for significant recovery to occur. If there is a very severe injury to the neural tube in which the axons run, complete recovery may not occur, resulting in permanent weakness.

Discussion

Brachial plexus injuries are far more common than realized. A study of the 1976 University of Wisconsin and the 1974 United States Naval Academy football teams revealed that approximately 38% sustained at least one "burner" or grade I injury during that season. Fortunately, grade II injuries are far less common; they do occur, however, and are frequently missed because the athletes do not develop complete paralysis. These athletes instead have varying degrees of weakness which could predispose them to far more serious injury.

An in-depth study of over 40 grade II injuries presented to the University of Wisconsin Sports Medicine Center reveals that the injury involves almost exclusively the nerve fibers to the supra- and infraspinatus, the deltoid, the subscapularis, and the biceps muscles, and very occasionally, the common extensor muscles. Because the plexus is composed of numerous paths, the only common site where all these fibers can be found is the upper trunk. Injury to the upper trunk is most likely to occur when the shoulder is forced either downward or backward while the head is either extended or flexed away from the involved shoulder. This mechanism is frequently seen in blocking or tackling, or when one falls and lands simultaneously on the side of the head and the point of the shoulder, as seen occasionally in wrestling.

After sustaining an injury in which there were symptoms of numbness, tingling, and/or burning pain radiating down the arm, one must do a complete neuromuscular exam of the neck, shoulder, and arm to determine whether there has been any neck or brachial plexus injury. Neck pain along with muscle weakness is a sign that there may be a fracture or dislocation of the cervical spine, as true neck pain is rarely associated with plexus injury, and appropriate medical care and transport should be employed.

Peripheral Nerve Injuries About the Shoulder

The peripheral nerves located at or near the base of the neck may be injured during participation in sport. Injuries to these nerves are indeed rare and usually occur as the result of a blow by some external object. The spinal accessory nerve, which innervates the trapezius muscle, is very superficial as it exits from behind the sternocleidomastoid muscle before entering the trapezius muscle. Injury to this nerve results in weakness on lifting the arm. There will be weakness on shoulder shrug and there may even be a rotatory winging of the scapula.

The suprascapular nerve which innervates the supra- and infraspinatus muscles may also be injured by a direct blow or may be injured by traction when the shoulder and scapula are forced downward and backward. The injury results in weakness in abduction and elevation of the shoulder. The long thoracic nerve which innervates the serratus anterior muscle may likewise be injured by a blow to the base of the neck resulting in winging of the scapula.

Axillary nerve injury may also occur as the result of a direct blow leading to marked weakness of the deltoid muscle. Additionally, axillary and/or musculocutaneous nerve injury may occur as a result of an anterior shoulder dislocation. Consequently, neurological examination should be performed before and after shoulder reduction.

In each case an EMG, if performed 2 to 3 weeks after the injury, will distinguish these from a plexus injury and delineate the seriousness. If recovery has not been noted within 6 months, surgical exploration should be considered.

Acromioclavicular Injuries

Acromioclavicular injuries may occur by two different mechanisms. The first involves a fall where one lands on the point of the shoulder, which may produce a first, second, or third degree injury. With this mechanism the acromion, coracoid, and scapula as well as the clavicle are driven downwards. The excursion of the clavicle is limited by the first rib. If the force continues the A-C joint undergoes failure, followed by failure of the coracoclavicular ligaments.

The second mechanism consists of a fall on an outstretched arm. This mechanism will generally only produce a first or second degree injury. It is extremely uncommon to produce a third degree injury by falling on an outstretched arm because the fall drives the scapula upward and backward; thus the coracoid process moves up toward the clavicle. If the force continues to drive the scapula backward, the load is first sustained by the A-C joint. Since the coracoid travels parallel to the clavicle in this injury, the coracoclavicular ligaments seldom undergo complete failure. There tends to be some compression of the A-C joint with this injury, however, which may lead to a meniscal injury.

A first degree injury consists of a mild partial ligament failure of the A-C joint without any injury of the coracoclavicular ligaments. The injury usually produces only very mild pain with shoulder motion, but may be increased with forced shoulder adduction. There is no increased motion of the A-C joint.

A mild or moderate second degree A-C joint injury consists of partial injury to the A-C joint and the coracoacromial ligaments. In a severe grade II injury there is complete A-C joint disruption and partial injury to the coracoacromial ligaments. In the former instance, there is pain to palpation of the A-C joint and the coracoid process, but there is very minimal increased motion at the A-C joint. In the latter case, there is significant increased motion of the A-C joint in the horizontal plane and some in the vertical plane. In either case, there is pain to palpation of both the A-C joint and the coracoid process, as well as pain with shoulder motion, most noticeable with adduction.

X-rays should be taken when there is an A-C joint injury to differentiate between a fracture or joint disruption. The X-ray request should state that the X-ray is of the A-C joint and not the shoulder, as shoulder X-rays are usually taken with the patient lying supine. Even if the athlete has a complete A-C separation, X-rays taken while lying down may not demonstrate it. A-C joint X-rays should be taken of both shoulders, with weights hanging from the forearms.

The X-rays of a first degree injury will be normal, whereas there may be some mild elevation in those with a second degree injury depending on the severity of injury to the A-C joint. With a third degree injury, meaning complete disruption of both the A-C joint and the coracoacromial ligaments, there will be significant elevation of the clavicle above the acromion. The amount of elevation is dependent upon the tear between the trapezius and deltoid muscle junction over the distal end of the clavicle.

Treatment

Treatment of a first degree injury is totally symptomatic. This usually consists of a sling for several days, followed by Codman's pendulum exercises, followed by progressive resistive exercises. Return to competition is allowed when there is full range of motion versus resistance, particularly with adduction. Treatment of a second degree sprain follows the same program except in those who have sustained a complete A-C joint injury. In these cases, one may desire to utilize a Kenny-Howard type of immobilizer for 3 weeks before starting the rehabilitation program.

Treatment of grade III injury is still the subject of controversy. There are a number who recommend surgical repair, and a equal number who recommend 6 weeks of total immobilization. Although few in number, some recommend early mobilization and rehabilitation, accepting the deformity.

The surgical procedures consist of either K-wire fixation of the A-C joint, circumferential wiring of the clavicle and coracoid process, which requires later removal of the wire, the use of a merciline tape instead of wire, fixation of the clavicle to the coracoid by a screw, transfer of the coracoid process to the clavicle, or resection of the outer end of the clavicle and transfer of the coracoacromial ligament to the clavicle. These procedures usually require 6 weeks of shoulder immobilization. All of these procedures will yield good results.

Conservative treatment consists of 6 weeks of total immobilization with a Kenny-Howard sling. X-rays are taken at 3 days and then at weekly intervals until the fourth week to see that reduction is maintained. At 6 weeks Codman's exercises are begun, followed by a progressive resistance weight program. It must be added that after removal of the immobilization device, it is not uncommon to note that there is some mild subluxation of the A-C joint.

When there is gross cosmetic deformity, surgical repair should be the treatment of choice. When there is just a little deformity due to sustaining only a minimal tear in the deltoid-trapezius muscle junction, however, early functional rehabilitation is our treatment of choice, and the results have been most gratifying.

Early traumatic arthritis has been seen in a number of our cases and has been reported by others. This is rarely seen in those with third degree injuries, but rather in those with first and second degree injuries. I believe that this is a result of a meniscal injury which occurred at the time of injury. Further studies indicate that this is more likely to occur in those injuries in which compression occurred at the A-C joint, such as a fall on the outstretched arm. It is doubtful that any particular type of treatment would prevent this.

Sternoclavicular Injuries

Although uncommon in most sports, sternoclavicular injuries are not infrequently seen in wrestlers. Posterior dislocation can be a life-threatening injury.

Sternoclavicular injury is usually a result of a fall on the outstretched hand while the body is rotating in the opposite direction. This may result in a first or second degree joint injury and rarely in an anterior dislocation or fracture dislocation of the epiphysis which may not close until age 19.

Routine X-ray interpretation of the sternoclavicular joint is difficult. To determine if there is a subluxation, dislocation, or epiphyseal fracture dislocation, a supine film of the sternoclavicular joint is taken with the X-ray tube angled 40° cephalad. If the injured S-C joint shows the clavicle to be higher than the uninjured side, the clavicle is dislocated anteriorly; similarly, if the clavicle is inferior in respect to its opposite side then it is dislocated posteriorly.

Treatment of first and second degree injuries consists of immobilization in a sling. If there is a great deal of pain, a figure of eight immobilizer, generally used for a fractured clavicle, is also utilized. This figure of eight is the treatment of choice for complete sternoclavicular dislocation.

A posterior dislocation may become a life-threatening situation as the proximal dislocated clavicle may compress the trachea. The arm should be abducted and traction outward is applied. This should reduce the dislocation. A complete dislocation should be maintained in a reduced state for at least 6 weeks, as recurrent or persistent dislocations yield very poor results on reconstruction. Treatment and rehabilitation programs for first, second, and third degree sternoclavicular injuries are similar to those used for acromioclavicular injuries.

Shoulder Dislocations

Although recurrent anterior shoulder dislocations rarely lead to severe traumatic arthritis, they present a significant functional problem. The exact cause of recurrence is as yet not fully understood. The various causes for the recurrence have been attributed to: (a) inadequate healing of the torn anterior inferior capsule and labrum; (b) the Hill-Sachs lesion in the humeral head which is a compression fracture of the posterior lateral humeral head due to its impingement on the anterior glenoid at the time of dislocation. When the arm is abducted and externally rotated there is no longer congruity of the humeral head with the glenoid due to the defect in the head, the "Hill-Sachs lesion," and the head will slip forward; (c) a tear of the rotator cuff; (d) increased forward angulation of the glenoid; and (e) neuromuscular imbalance between the subscapularis and the external rotator muscles. Although the exact cause or causes are not known, it has been well documented that those with a large humeral head defect have a higher incidence of recurrence.

Rowe's study of 145 patients with recurrent shoulder dislocations revealed that there was only one factor that correlated with recurrence and that was the age of the patient at the time of initial injury. The recurrence rate for those under age 20 was 83%; for those between the ages of 20 and 40 years it was 63%, and for those over age 40 it was 16%.

For individuals under 40 who sustain their first episode of anterior dislocation, the usual method of treatment is 3 to 6 weeks of total shoulder immobilization. Our usual treatment consists of 3 weeks of total immobilization followed by Codman's exercises, progressing to active assisted, and then to a formal weight training program. We are, however, reevaluating this period of immobilization in some of these patients. Since the recurrence rate is so high in spite of an adequate period of immobilization, we start selected athletes in this age group on a very early functional rehabilitation program. Interestingly, over the past 4 years, five University of Wisconsin football players who sustained their first episode of dislocation and who were treated for a minimum of 3 weeks of strict immobilization followed by a well controlled and supervised weight program had recurrence within 1½ years.

Posterior dislocations rarely occur in contact sports, and when they do, they often go unrecognized. Frequently, only an anterior-posterior X-ray is taken and is misinterpreted as showing a normal shoulder joint. Axillary view, a transthoracic lateral, or other lateral views of the glenoid must be obtained in all suspected dislocations in order to properly evaluate this joint. Clinically posterior dislocations or impacted posterior subluxations are to be highly suspected when external rotation is not possible with attempts at gentle passive external rotation of the arm.

Recurrent Traumatic Subluxation/Dislocations

Traumatic recurrent subluxations in my experience are probably a more common problem in athletes than recurrent dislocations. Frequently the athlete has had an initial episode of dislocation, either requiring formal reduction or one that spontaneously reduced. Their chief complaint is posterior lateral shoulder pain after each episode of subluxation. Although this posterior lateral shoulder pain has been attributed to pain from the Hill-Sachs lesion, the pain may indeed be supra- and/or infraspinatus muscle pain due to an excessive spontaneous contraction of these muscles to produce shoulder reduction. Once anterior shoulder subluxation occurs, subscapularis muscle contraction may cause dislocation. Although it has been taught that subscapularis muscle strengthening may prevent dislocation, one must consider that with a stretched anterior inferior capsule, subluxation may occur before the proprioceptors in the capsule can be stretched to stimulate subscapularis firing. If the head is on the glenoid rim, any firing of the subscapularis will probably cause a dislocation. Biomechanically, only the supraspinatus and infraspinatus muscles can prevent the dislocation; thus it would seem that it would be extremely important to strengthen these muscles in those with a history of recurrent subluxation or dislocation.

Overuse Injuries About the Shoulder

Shoulder impingement is the most common problem about the shoulder encountered in our Sports Medicine Clinic. Shoulder impingement syndrome has also been called supraspinatus syndrome, pitchers' shoulder, tennis shoulder, and swimmers' shoulder. The exact pathophysiology is as yet unknown, but it is theorized that there are several factors that may play a part in the etiology. It has been shown that adduction and internal rotation with the shoulder at 90° of elevation leads to marked decrease in blood flow to the rotator cuff. Accumulated microtrauma to the cuff as seen in the arduous workouts in swimmers, combined with poor cuff blood supply, could lead to secondary supraspinatus bursa inflammation. A thickened bursa will further compromise the minimal space between the greater tuberosity of the humerus and the anterior acromion and the entrapped coracoacromial ligament. With a chronically inflamed bursa any shoulder motion at 90° will continue the inflammatory process producing a vicious cycle. It is possible that in some or even many cases the only pathology present is a chronically inflamed supraspinatus bursa (subdeltoid bursa), a result of repetitive mechanical irritation.

Because shoulder impingement syndrome is so difficult to treat, it is important to try to prevent the entity. The first line of defense is setting up a strength and flexibility program designed specifically for the sport involved. The second is to design a training program which does not severely overload the shoulder, has periods of hard training alternating with periods of decreased training, and at all times maintains a flexibility program.

Once the injury occurs, the physical exam will reveal tenderness to palpation of the anterior rotator cuff just in front of the acromion. There will be pain and apprehension when the examiner abducts the arm to 90° and then passively circumducts the arm and shoulder across the chest, or when the shoulder and arm while at 90° are just adducted and internally rotated. Treatment consists of rest, localized heat, oral anti-inflammatory agents, and a flexibility program. If there is no relief of symptoms within 2 to 3 weeks, or if the symptoms have been present longer than 6 weeks, a soluble steroid is injected into the supraspinatus bursa (subdeltoid bursa).

In cases resistant to treatment, or in those with frequent recurrence, excision of the coracoacromial ligament and the subdeltoid bursa may be indicated. The results of surgery in these cases have yielded reasonably high success rates. When biceps tendonitis is noted to be associated with shoulder impingement, conservative treatment may be expected to take a much longer time. The surgical results of decompression alone are also disappointing when chronic biceps tendonitis is present.

Biceps tendonitis is most commonly found in association with shoulder impingement syndrome; however, we are seeing more and more cases occurring as isolated overuse injuries. Primary biceps tendonitis is seen most commonly as a result of weight training programs, most frequently associated with bench and incline presses. Treatment consists of refraining from bench presses and any shoulder functions occurring at 90° of abduction. Localized heat, stretching, and oral anti-inflammatory agents are used, and only in cases of chronicity are soluble steroids utilized.

The Athletic Foot and Its Import to Performance During Running

Richard Bogdan
California College of Podiatric Medicine

The foot is the link between the ground or level of support and the rest of the body. This statement is exemplified in sports, and in particular, running, which lends itself to malpositioning of the joints. Malpositioning may produce overuse symptoms, whereas adequate control of the motions about a joint creates a more perfect form and enables the athlete to excel.

Much has been gleaned by observing high speed films and relating them to foot types. Classifying feet by the classical methods as flat, normal, and high arched is common, but podiatrists have developed a more sensitive classification correlating joint positions of the major joints of the foot to the classical appearances. The major joints of the foot are the subtalar, mid tarsal, first ray, and the ankle joint. The joint orientations are examined in all three of the body planes.

Problems and Conditions of the Foot

The flat foot is a major concern in sports because it is quite common and seems to develop the largest amount of pathology and symptoms. Podiatry has found the etiology of the flat foot due to a condition of the mid tarsal joint called fore foot varus. With fore foot varus, the inside front part of the foot is elevated when the subtalar joint is in its ideal, that is, neutral, position. To bring the fore foot to the ground, the heel must turn in and the arch collapses. This causes other position changes as far up as the back.

A tight achilles tendon is another major condition of the foot which

Richard Bogdan, DPM, MS, is a sports podiatrist and professor at the California College of Podiatric Medicine in Concord, California.

causes an excessive toe-walking condition and stress on the mid foot. This condition, caused or aggravated by athletics, will make the arch collapse or lower. A leg condition, Genu varum or bowleggedness, also will cause the arch to flatten so that the foot lies flat to the ground for stability.

Podiatrists have found that any hypermobility of a joint in the mid foot area (or distal to it) will have a foot-flattening effect. The degree to which this occurs is relative to the height of the arch and the subsequent foot and limb compensation requirements.

The ideal foot has a moderate arch morphology, where the heel is perpendicular to the ground and in line with the leg bisection. Also, the leg is perpendicular to the ground, and the fore foot is perpendicular to the bisection of the heel in a nonweight-bearing position. This foot has no pathology or symptoms.

The high-arched foot is called a pes cavus foot. This foot is developmental either by the congenital position of the foot from birth or compensation of the foot. The condition most commonly seen is due to the fore foot valgus foot type, where the front part of the foot is tilted downward on the inside, as compared to the outside, part of the foot. This causes the back of the heel to invert or tilt outward when the individual stands on the foot.

The reason for discussing types of feet is to describe the differences in gait. The normal gait pattern of the foot during stance phase begins with heel contact and ends with the toe-off. The foot will pronate or the arch roll in in the early phases of gait and will supinate (roll out) in the latter phases of gait. The pronation motion of the foot adapts the foot to the ground and takes up shock. After the foot has performed this phase, it requires rigidity for propulsion to leave the ground in the most efficient way.

Podiatrists evaluate the gait motions from the posterior aspect of the heel. The heel is tilted outward at the time of contact and pronates to become tilted inward (everted) when the foot is flat on the ground. It slowly tilts outward when the forces are on the fore foot during resupination of the foot (rigid lever stage).

In running, the gait differs by the placement of the foot according to the speed at which one runs, the sport, and the age of the athlete. The foot is in a phase of longer pronation for the adaptation and shock absorption thrust upon it. Depending on the activity, shock to the foot can be up to six gravities (G). The speed of the runner also varies where the contact is to be made on the foot. The jogger lands on the lateral heel and mid foot, the middle distance runner lands more on the mid foot and ball, and the sprinter lands on the ball of the foot. The sprinter's position enables the foot to be less in contact with the ground and produces more forward speed.

The age of the athlete can be a factor in running gait. For example, a youngster's neuromuscular coordination and form may not yet be perfected. The older athlete could have poor form, previous injuries, or contractural muscular states that cause aberrations to the placement of the foot.

The running gait differs from that of walking in that the foot is placed on or over the line of progression. This develops an outward, angular tilt of the limb (of a large varus degree at times). The limb varus position compensates at the midtarsal joint of the foot to absorb this extra amount of limb tilt. When the support limb singly has the force of 3 Gs placed upon it, along with a large varus tilt, more pronation and prolonged pronation of the foot is required.

The foot's compensation for extra tilt causes excessive movement of leg bones as well as foot bones. The muscles and ligaments helping to support the foot and limb will overwork and excessive fatigue or stress occurs. If one places an abnormal foot condition or limb condition in the above running formula, severe demands occur on this system. Malfunction occurs with symptoms from the foot to the hips. The following will describe common symptoms in the foot and their etiology as related to foot function.

The achilles tendonitis is related to poor shock absorption found in both the pes cavus foot and the pronated foot. The pronated foot will shorten the achilles tendon muscle complex, allowing strain and stress on the tendon. Most athletes have a tightened posterior muscle group which will aggravate any existing condition.

The heel spur syndrome is usually a bursitis, nerve inflammation, or fascial strain about the heel. This is found in flat-footed persons because of their excessive pronation and the resulting strain on this area. Individuals with high arches also have this condition, however. The explanation is that the plantar fascia, a major supporting factor of the high arch, will strain with any mild excessive stress to the foot, although the flat foot is more strained than the high-arched foot.

Digital problems, such as ingrown or black toe nails, blisters, corns, and hammer toes, are from the inadequate toe box height or length when the foot goes through its longer phase of pronation. In a "C" shaped shoe, the foot knocks against the outside of the shoe when it pronates.

Pain between toes is usually caused by a pinched nerve or a benign nerve tumor called a neuroma and can make a foot feel like a hot poker. This condition is found with a foot that pronates excessively, causing the metatarsal heads to rub together excessively as well.

When the bony structures of the foot experience excessive microtrauma, they try to remodel themselves to the new stress. If the stress is accumulated too fast, the matrix of the bone will break down and a stress fracture occurs. The lack of shock absorption of both foot types can cause this to occur; in fact, even a normal foot can experience a stress fracture. The pes cavus foot type is more likely to have this condition, however.

Shin splints are related to the excessive foot pronation of the flat foot. The most common site of shin splints is the posterior medial muscle groups, which decelerate pronation, followed by the anterior muscle groups, which attempt to decelerate the foot from slapping the ground.

One can also correlate poor mechanics in the foot to running syndromes in the legs and thigh. One of the most prevalent syndromes of the lower limbs is the overuse injuries of the knee. These injuries occur inside, outside, under, above, below, and behind the knee. The majority of the knee injuries are inflammatory in origin or due to excessive compression of the cartilage of the knee cap. Meniscal cartilage tears are rare, but they still occur and should be looked for. The overuse of the tendons trying to support the knee joint occur via the increase of the Q angle or Genu Valgum during a sport activity. The excessive pronation of the foot, along with poor osseous structure about the knee, aggravates the normal positions of running limbs. Most of the knee symptoms related to pronation are medial capsular pain, Pes Anserinus Syndrome, medial hamstring, and early patellar compression syndrome. Lateral knee pain about the patella is due to rapid pronation of the foot. Some lateral knee pains, however, are due to the lack of shock absorption of the foot in the rigid pes cavus foot type. This is normally seen in the lateral collateral ligament or the insertional area of the iliotibial band. Poor flexibility about the knee can cause superior/inferior and posterior symptomatology.

The iliotibial band syndrome is classically a frictional rubbing of the band across the greater trochanter of the femur. This may occur in association with either excessive or normal pronation during a fatigue state. The excessive pronated position of the foot causes excessive internal rotation of the femur and if the tensor fascia lata is straining, it will become a tight band. The great trochanter then rubs underneath this band, causing an inflammation. Excessive shock to a limb can also create tightness in the lateral thigh musculature, and normal rotation then can create inflamed areas of the iliotibial band.

Leg stress fractures are again associated with foot types that have poor shock absorption.

One of the most perplexing structural aberrations is the syndrome of limb length difference. About 90 percent of the population has a limb length difference of 1/8 to 1/2 inch. With normal walking, only minimal symptoms or compensations may be seen. But with running, the functional stress placed on the limbs increases about 3 to 6 times. Obviously, then, overuse syndromes of all types and at different joint levels occur.

The limb length differences can be due to the malfunction of one foot to the contralateral side. One foot can pronate more during stance than the other foot, causing this limb to be shorter than the other. Symptoms are probably less above the knees than with the anatomical structural problem.

Low back symptoms such as fatigue, sciatica, and arthritis can be associated or compounded by the foot imbalances. Compensated foot position lends to poor shock absorption and thus to more shock to the back and hip area. Proper foot and limb function will help reduce the symptoms of fatigue, sciatica, and arthritis—and probably will prevent them from occurring in the first place.

To treat injuries to the foot, the injured part must first be immobilized in order to reduce inflammation. Immobilization rests the injured part; rest may be total or minimal movement or another sport activity that does not stress the injured part. Inflammation may also be reduced with ice or medication.

The next stage of treatment is mild mobilization of the joints about the injured part. The stretching decreases spasm and weakness of musculature. The strengthening of the part is created by motion with minimal stress; that is, first through isometric activity, then isotonic or isokinetic exercises.

If the injury evaluation has revealed foot or limb imbalance, this should be corrected to enable faster healing and future prevention of the disorder. Strapping the foot with tape and padding demonstrates the need for a permanent functional orthotic or shoe modification.

Field Examination of the Athlete's Foot and Leg

Complete examination of the lower extremity is a complex process which involves the history of any sports-related symptoms or injuries, examination of structure, function, gait patterns, shoe wear patterns, skin callus locations. Often X-rays or laboratory tests are needed to confirm a diagnosis.

Stance Position Examination

Have an individual wearing shorts stand barefoot in his or her normal angle and base of gait; that is, the angle of the foot from the direction of motion and the distance between the ankles while walking and running. The person should stand relaxed with equal weight on each foot. Normally, each foot makes a 10° angle with the line of progression, and the width between the ankles is about 3''. In stance, with the body erect and arms resting at the sides, the hips, pelvis, and shoulders should be level, the spine straight, and the head erect. Then, check for the following:

1. The center of the knee joint should be over the center of the ankle

joint.

2. There should be no bowlegs or knockknees.

3. The heel bone should be in line with the lower leg and straight (perpendicular) to the ground.

4. The ball of the foot should be flat on the ground, the toes straight and parallel with each other (no bunions, hammertoes, or pressure points from shoe initiation).

5. The inside arch should form a smooth curve.

The person should be able to stand in this position comfortably with no foot fatigue or low back strain for at least 5 minutes. If a structural imbalance exists, muscles try to compensate with resulting fatigue. The most common problems seen in stance are bowed legs, tilted heel bone, flat feet, and contracted tendons to the toes.

The One-Foot Test

The ability to balance on one foot is a good test for structural and muscular stability. The person should be able to balance on one foot for at least 3 minutes; there should be a balance between the inside muscles (anterior and posterior tibial), outside muscles (peroneus longus and brevis), and between the front muscles (anterior tibial and extensor digitorum longus) and back muscles of the calf. Weight stress constantly falling to the inside indicates a mobile, pronated foot type that needs support. If weight stress falls to the outside, causing inversion of the foot, then the range of motion at the joints is not sufficient for normal function, and needs either stretching exercises, external support, or both. This test will also indicate the general laxity or tightness of joints for the individual and explain how they might function under stress.

Off Weight-Bearing Examination

This examination must be performed from a number of angles. First, examine the foot from the bottom, looking for any corns, calluses, blisters, or skin irritations. These conditions will indicate tissue stress and possible imbalance. Then, observe the foot from the top for any tight tendons, crooked deformed toes, corns, or pressure points on toenails, all of which could become disabling during competition.

Next, with the person seated or lying supine on the back, check to see if s/he can perform the following:

1. The legs should be able to rotate in or out equally, and the resting position from the knee joint should be straight ahead.

2. The legs should extend fully straight, with no stress on the hamstring muscles.

3. With the knee straight, the foot should be able to move up at least

$10°$ at the ankle joint to form an angle of about $80°$ with the lower leg.

Finally, have the individual lie prone (face down), with the knees straight, and the feet hanging at rest, and check for the following:

1. The ball of the foot should be perpendicular or tilted slightly inward (less than $5°$) from the direction of the heel bone.

2. The heel bone should be in line or tilted slightly inward (less than $5°$) from the lower part of the leg.

Summary

A small degree of imbalance of the foot or leg will cause compensatory muscle strain, leading to overuse injury during a conditioning program. This overuse may show on the skin, deeper soft structures, or even bone (i.e., stress fractures). Prevention of overuse injuries is successful with proper examination, training for flexibility and strength, and the use of supportive protective footgear. Traumatic injuries need time to heal, but overuse injuries can be evaluated and treated without disability and lost training time. A few minutes of examination early in the conditioning program may prevent a season of nagging injuries.

Eye Injuries - The A-B-C's and a Few X-Y-Z's for the Athletic Trainer

Lee R. Minton
Eye Physicians Center

Sport-related eye injury has reached epidemic proportions in this country. Statistics from the National Society to Prevent Blindness indicate that over 100,000 significant athletic injuries occur yearly. As a result, 25% suffer severe ocular complications. Athletics account for 23% of eye injuries seen at the Massachusetts Eye and Ear Infirmary. No sport is immune to these injuries. Hockey in particular had the highest percentage of ocular injuries per participant until face-protective standards cut this dramatically a few years ago. The culprit now is racquet sports, due to the increased interest in racquetball and tennis during the past decade. Eye injuries from baseball, basketball, boxing, and soccer follow close behind.

For athletes, sight is the most precious of the five senses. Athletic trainers must be aware of their responsibility to the athlete to protect this vital sense. Therefore, it is imperative that athletic trainers have some basic understanding of ocular anatomy in addition to their knowledge of the basic anatomy of the knee or shoulder. The athletic trainer must know the common signs and symptoms of eye injury, should be competent in immediate eye care, should have an emergency eye care kit, and should use common sense in deciding which injury should be referred to the ophthalmologist. The first person caring for an eye injury has a large measure of responsibility for the ultimate salvage of the eye. Of vital importance in handling the ocular athletic injury is a knowledgeable approach, a cool head, and some common sense.

In caring for the injured eye, as with any injury, the trainer must know the history and present status. How was the injury received? What is the

Lee Minton, MD, FACS, is an ophthalmologist at the Eye Physicians Center in Nashville, Tennessee.

visual status? Is there pain or double vision? After asking the athlete about the injury and the symptoms, the trainer should examine the eye for various conditions. For example, he or she should examine for such things as the condition of the lids, checking for conjunctiva hyperemic, and the condition of the cornea, for abrasions or lacerations. The trainer should be sure there is no blood in the anterior chamber, and finally, the condition of the pupil should be noted.

Hyphema

This term refers to blood in the aqueous area between the posterior portion of the cornea and the iris, the anterior chamber. Even a trace of blood in this area is highly significant. The bleeding results from disruption of small blood vessels where the root of the iris inserts into the ciliary body. This finding may be present in any eye injury. The hyphema usually causes pain, which in some cases is extreme, along with marked hyperemia of the conjunctiva. The athlete's vision will be blurred, and if the hyphema completely fills the anterior chamber, the athlete may not be able to see light. Usually at the onset, there is a small amount of blood which settles to the bottom of the anterior chamber.

In all types of eye injuries, the anterior chamber should be examined closely with a bright light. If blood is detected in the anterior chamber, both eyes should be patched and a shield taped over the injured eye. The athlete should have no activity and be transported to an ophthalmologist immediately. Hospitalization, with bedrest, usually is suggested for 5 days with both eyes patched. No other treatment is indicated except sedation and treatment for pain if necessary. Without bedrest, there is considerable chance that the eye will continue to bleed. In any case, all athletes who have suffered a hyphema should be kept out of contact sports for an indefinite time depending on the condition of the eye. Also, the presence of blood in the anterior chamber may cause much drowsiness by an unexplained mechanism. Although the hyphema alone may cause the drowsiness and lack of alertness, the possibility of head injury should be considered.

Again, bedrest is vital with hyphema, for secondary bleeding is much more serious than the initial bleeding. If the initial or secondary bleeding has completely filled the anterior chamber, approximately 35% of those injured will finally have visual acuity of less than 20/40. Although most of these hyphemas can be treated conservatively, about 8% require surgical intervention. Surgical intervention is indicated when the eye has developed an "eight ball" appearance, with the anterior chamber taking on a dark chocolate appearance. This sign indicates that a dense clot has developed, with accompanying elevation of intraocular pressure. In some of these cases, the eye must be opened and the clot washed out. The tragedy of hyphemas is that about 7% of such patients develop "recession angle deformity" glaucoma sometime in the future. The hyphema-type injury may also be accompanied by hemorrhage within the vitreous, hemorrhage in the retina, or even a dislocated lens.

Another complication with hyphema is the possibility of a traumatic disinsertion of the iris from the ciliary body. This results from the iris root being pulled from the ciliary body. A sign of this injury is a crescent-shaped "extra pupil" noted peripherally where the iris inserts. In these cases, the pupil is usually decentered.

Abrasion of the Cornea

Because of the great number of sensory nerves in the cornea, this external injury results in extreme pain. If the abrasion is extensive, there may be some visual disturbance. The conjunctiva will react immediately with hyperemia and reddening of the eye from dilated vessels.

If this injury is suspected, a sterile topical anesthetic should be applied, then a sterile fluorescein strip touched to the inside of the lower lid so that a blue light can help detect staining of the cornea. If a corneal abrasion is found, a broad spectrum antibiotic such as Neosporin or Statrol should be dropped in the eye and the athlete should be referred to an ophthalmologist. It should then be treated with a topical, broad spectrum antibiotic every 1 or 2 hours for 2 or 3 days to prevent corneal ulceration. No topical anesthetic and no drops containing steroid solution should be used because this will delay healing of the abrasion and may precipitate a viral ulcer of the cornea.

With a large corneal abrasion, the ciliary muscle may go into spasm and the pupil constrict. The pupil must then be dilated with homatropine for several hours until the abrasion heals. Some patients experience less pain if the eye is patched whereas other patients prefer no patch. Either way is fine, for no evidence suggests that patching the eye makes the abrasion heal more quickly. The most serious complication resulting from an abrasion is a corneal ulcer, which may damage vision. A less serious complication is recurrent erosion, which may develop weeks after apparent healing. Recurrent erosion is particularly common with finger-nail injury to the cornea.

Subconjunctival Hemorrhage

Any ocular trauma may rupture small conjunctival veins, resulting in a bright red accumulation of blood under the conjunctiva almost immediately after the injury. Although this sign may be associated with other injuries, the subconjunctival hemorrhage frequently is the only manifestation of injury. In the absence of other injuries, these patients experience no pain or loss of vision. This condition need not be referred and requires no treatment. Only if there are significant signs and symptoms along with a subconjunctival hemorrhage should the athlete be referred to an ophthalmologist.

Traumatic Iritis

The most common cause of traumatic iritis, which may accompany any injury to the eye, is the compression-type injury which causes damage to the iris and ciliary body. The manifestation of the iritis may be immediate or delayed. The patient usually experiences a rather dull pain in the eye, blurred vision, and photosensitivity. Examination of the eye may or may not reveal a corneal abrasion, although there is usually some hyperemia of the conjunctiva. The eyes' natural reaction to this injury is a spasm of the iris muscles, causing the pupil to become constricted. In some cases the pupil dilates due to trauma to the sphincter muscle. Without question these cases should be referred for further examination and treatment. If the iritis is the only finding, treatment consists of topical steroid drops and dilation of the pupil with homatropine drops. Patients should wear dark glasses for the photosensitivity.

Lacerations of the Eyelids and Brows

Small, superficial lacerations of the eyelids do not require suturing because the healing is usually prompt and leaves no scar. These lacerations should be cleaned with a sterilizing soap, then closed with tape such as Steri-Strip. If the laceration is extensive, the athlete should be referred to a physician for suturing and immunization for tetanus. The eye lashes may be trimmed if necessary; regrowth takes place in a few days. The eyebrow should not be shaved, however, for eyebrow hair often will not regrow or will grow back irregularly.

Eyelid Margin Lacerations

All lacerations around the lid should be inspected closely to determine if the eyelid margin is involved. Patients with this injury should be referred to an ophthalmologist or plastic surgeon for repair, because otherwise a notch in the lid may cause a cosmetic blemish or tearing. Of particular importance are the lid margin lacerations which involve the lower tear duct opening and canal. If this unimpressive appearing laceration is not found and sutured properly, the patient may experience chronic tearing.

Traumatic Retinal Detachment

A retinal detachment exists when the retina has become separated from the underlying vascular layer, the choroid. Usually this is manifested by a retinal hole or a disinsertion where the retina attaches peripherally, with a serous fluid forming between the retina and choroid. If the detachment is left unrepaired, the eye invariably loses all sight.

It is estimated that a contusion-type trauma is involved in 15% to 20% of all retinal detachments. The detachment usually occurs later than the trauma; 80% are found within 2 years of the injury, although some do occur at the time of the ocular contusion. The incidence of traumatic detachment is higher in the near-sighted athlete. Retinal detachment symptoms are "flashing lights" in darkness, "floating black specks," and sometimes a "veil or curtain" visual sensation.

Retinal detachment requires surgical treatment. Most retinal surgeons allow the athletes to return to competition after retinal detachment surgery, provided the athlete knows the possible consequences. Boxers, highly near-sighted athletes, or athletes with a blind or amblyopic opposite eye might be an exception.

Superficial Foreign Body

Foreign material in the form of particles may be in the conjunctival cul-de-sac, on the cornea, or under the eyelid. In some instances, the foreign body is embedded in the cornea. To examine and treat this injury, the athlete should be seated while the trainer examines the eye with a good light. The foreign material may be located after application of a drop or two of topical anesthetic. If examination under the upper lid is necessary, the upper lid should be everted. To evert the eyelid, the trainer should have the patient look down, and then should grasp the central upper lid lashes and pull slightly outward and down. The trainer—or examiner—should then press inward the central portion of the upper lid with a cotton applicator, Q-tip, finger, or even a bent tobacco pipe cleaner, flipping the upper lid over. The foreign body may be irrigated with a solution such as Eye Stream or mopped out with a moistened Q-tip or cotton applicator. The removal of an embedded foreign body should be followed by a drop of a broad spectrum antibiotic such as Neosporin or Statrol.

Traumatic Cataracts and Dislocated Lens

A laceration and contusion of the globe may cause an opacity of the crystalline lens. This condition is usually accompanied by other injuries to the eye. A cataractous lens may not develop until years after the initial injury. Because this condition greatly limits vision, cataract extraction may be required. Athletic injury may also cause the lens to become dislocated from its central position, and this frequently results in a cataractous lens. Dislocated lenses must be surgically removed, for an unremoved dislocated lens causes the intraocular pressure to rise, perhaps producing secondary glaucoma.

"Black Eye"

Blunt trauma or semiblunt trauma compresses the eye against the bony wall of the orbit in spite of the protective fatty pad between the eye and orbital walls. Depending on the nature of the injury, the athlete may experience moderate pain with transient visual loss or blurred vision. Almost immediately after the trauma, the lids swell from hemorrhage and edema. Several hours later, the opposite lid may become swollen and hemorrhagic. If there is a marked amount of bleeding, the eye may protrude forward. In some cases there may be double vision and ophthalmoplegia from hemorrhage into the muscles. The noncomplicated "black eye" can be treated with cold compresses in the form of a crushed eye pack to slow the bleeding. Crushed ice placed in a rubber glove makes an effective pack.

Fracture of Orbital Bones and
"Blowout" Fractures of the Orbital Floor

Any suspected fracture of the bones of the orbit should be referred for examination, X-ray, and treatment if necessary. Fractures of the roof of the orbit are usually not significant and require no treatment. Signs of this fracture are hemorrhage of the upper lid and/or subconjunctival hemorrhage. Fractures of the lateral wall of the orbit may avulse the optic nerve and cause profound loss of vision; this injury is very rare, however. Fracture of the medial wall produces signs and symptoms of air in the orbit because of the proximity of the paranasal sinuses. These injuries usually do not require surgical intervention, but their involvement with the sinuses requires some kind of systemic antibiotic.

Fractures of the orbital floor are more common and potentially more serious. When the force of a blunt object, such as a baseball, is exerted on the orbit, the orbital tissue compresses. The increased hydraulic pressure may result in a "blowout" fracture at the site of the weakest portion of the orbit, which is the paper-thin floor over the maxillary antrum. The orbital fat may prolapse into this sinus along with the inferior rectus and/or the inferior oblique muscle. When these two muscles are caught in the incarceration not only is their function restricted, but they also act as bands to prevent the full range of contraction of other ocular muscles not included in the fracture. As a result, upward gaze is often impaired. This occurs not only because of damage to the inferior oblique muscle but also because the superior rectus cannot elevate the globe against the short range of the entrapped inferior oblique muscle.

Clinical suspicion of the "blowout" fracture is based on one or more of the following findings: (a) anesthesia of the nose and skin of the lower lid; (b) double vision and limited motion of the inferior rectus and/or inferior oblique muscles; (c) pain on the affected side on upward gaze; and (d) hemorrhage and swelling into the orbit. The patient may or may not experience double vision from the onset of the injury. It should be remembered that the patient may experience double vision even without a floor fracture simply due to the hemorrhage into the orbit or into a muscle which limits ocular motility.

If after careful examination, there is any suspicion of a blowout fracture of the orbit, the patient should be referred. Further studies should include a tomography radiologic study. Routine X-ray study will give only a high percentage of false negative readings as opposed to the tomography, which is more accurate.

"Blowout" fractures, without symptoms, do not necessarily need surgical repair. If X-ray studies show marked incarceration of tissue and there is vertical limitation of ocular movement, then surgery should be performed within 2 or 3 weeks. Without surgery, the patient may suffer vertical diplopia. If these injuries are left untreated for an extended period of time, the surgical result may not be satisfactory and the athlete's double vision may continue.

Surgery for this injury consists of making an incision below the lower lid margin or through the skin along the lower orbital rim. The periosteum at the rim is incised horizontally and elevated from the bony orbital floor. The fracture is carefully defined by palpation and observation, the incarcerated tissue is removed, and entrapped muscles are released. If sufficient bone is not present for the floor restoration, then a sheet of Supramid material is placed between the periosteum and the bone fragments.

Protective Eye Gear

Sport-related ocular injuries can be diminished greatly by adequate protective eye gear. This was dramatically demonstrated when facial protective gear became a requirement for hockey players. Eye protection is particularly necessary in the racquet sports. The type of frame and lens selected will depend on the sport involved, the refractive error, and frame comfort. Corrective or noncorrective lens may be placed in an industrial-type frame made of polycarbonate material. This frame must have a posterior lip support for the inserted lens because a posterior lip will eject the lens forward on impact. The All-American frame (see Figure 1) made by Criss Company offers all these characteristics. The corrective lens should be made of polycarbonate material with a center thickness of at least 3 mms for best impact attenuation. Corrective or noncorrective lenses may also be placed in a plaster wrap-around frame such as Rainbo Eyeguard® (see Figure 2). A variety of excellent eye protectors are available for athletes who do not require corrective lenses or for those who wear contact lenses. These include Ektelon goggles® (see Figure 3) and the Pro-Tec PTE 500 eyeguard® (see Figure 4).

Athletic Trainer Eye Care Kit

An adequate ophthalmic first aid kit for the athletic trainer should include the following:
1. White light
2. Blue light
3. Sterile fluorescein strips
4. Sterile eye pads
5. Eye shield
6. Sterile cotton tip applicators
7. Topical anesthetic drops (Ophthetic)
8. Topical broad-spectrum antibiotic drops (Neosporin or Statrol)
9. Irrigating solution (Eye Stream)
10. Contact lens remover
11. Rubber glove (to be filled with crushed ice and used as a cold compress)

As stated earlier, the first person to treat an eye injury usually is the most responsible for salvaging the eye. And typically, athletic trainers will be that first person. So, with an understanding of the anatomy of the eye as well as familiarity with the above eye care kit and knowledge of how to use its components, athletic trainers will go a long way toward preventing and caring for eye injuries both in the field and in clinical settings.

Figure 1—*All-American Frame*. This frame is constructed of polycarbonate and may have corrective or noncorrective lens inserted. The frame is available with a hinged temple piece.

Figure 2—*Rainbo Eyeguard®*. Corrective, noncorrective, or no lens may be used in this polycarbonate frame. This frame offers a deep posterior lip to eject the lens forward on impact.

Figure 3—*Ektelon Goggle®* . This polycarbonate frame has wrap-around construction and does not limit peripheral vision. The lens has no correction.

Figure 4—*Pro-Tec PTE 500®* . This polycarbonate frame is excellent for athletes wearing contact lenses or for those not requiring corrective lenses.

Injuries to the Abdomen and Thorax: Diagnostic and Therapeutic Considerations

Kimball Maull
Medical College of Virginia Hospitals

Abdominal trauma does not occur only on the athletic field or court; it occurs in every walk of life. Statistics demonstrate that the major causes of accidental death in this country are motor vehicle accidents, falls, burns, and drownings. Note that sports injuries do not appear on this list of prominent accident causes. Yet, this does not minimize the importance of sports injuries. If we consider the number of injured, not just the number of fatalities, we find that 64 million people are injured per year. If the population of the U.S. is 220 million, this means that one individual in four is going to be injured to the extent that s/he will require medical care either in an emergency room or a physician's office. In 1976, 103,000 people were killed, 9 million were temporarily disabled, and 370,000 were permanently disabled, with a cost of 52.8 billion dollars. Trauma is the leading cause of death between the ages 1 and 44. Three-quarters of teen-age deaths and one-half of childhood deaths are caused by trauma.

Individuals suffering from sports injuries must be fitted into the emergency care system because he or she is likely to be the first person available to treat the injured athlete. The athletic trainer's responsibility to an injured player is unique in that the trainer must rapidly determine if that player has a serious injury and must make that assessment while keeping the available emergency care system in mind. The trainer must have the capability to communicate and to promptly evacuate the patient to a medical facility, one that will benefit the patient.

Kimball Maull, MD, is associate professor of surgery and director of Emergency Surgical Services at the Medical College of Virginia Hospitals in Richmond, Virginia.

Chest and Abdominal Injuries

What role do athletic trainers play when athletes suffer injuries to the chest and abdomen? First and most important, they must prevent further injuries to the patient. The second thing they must do is make a "patient assessment," that is, determine whether or not the patient has a serious injury. Frankly, the difficulties in making that assessment on the field are far greater than they are in the protected environment of an emergency room. The job of an athletic trainer is not an easy one.

What types of injuries can occur to the chest and abdomen? How can the athletic trainer decide whether or not a patient has a serious injury and what treatment the individual can be given until further medical assistance is available? Some chest injuries require immediate attention. Airway obstruction, without question, is the most significant problem and must be dealt with on a first priority basis. A finite number of injuries cause airway obstruction. For example, if the patient sustains a blow to the face and fractures the face, the patient may bleed or have teeth dislodged into the upper airway. Furthermore, if the patient is rendered unconscious and kept in the supine position, the tongue may fall back and obstruct the airway. Direct blows to the larynx and trachea are extremely serious and cause significant airway obstruction.

What should be done in this situation? First, the trainer must recognize what the consequences of an airway obstruction are. Obviously, interference with the normal air flow into and out of the lungs causes depletion of oxygen and buildup of carbon dioxide. The tissues do not receive enough oxygen and waste products accumulate, carbon dioxide rises, and the patient develops an acidosis. Further deterioration of the body chemistry occurs, with the patient eventually dying.

So as emphasized earlier, airway obstruction requires immediate treatment. Basically, an airway can be provided by simple means: Bringing the jaw forward will move the tongue away from the airway. Alternately, the trainer may place traction on the tongue and sweep the posterior pharynx with the fingers to remove blood, or loose dentures or food that might be obstructing the airway. Certain types of commercially available tubes, such as oro or nasopharyngeal tubes, can be placed directly into the upper air passages to maintain an open airway.

Also effective in treating airway obstruction is the head tilt maneuver. This technique may be dangerous, however, because it requires neck extension, and if the cervical spine is injured, the head-tilt maneuver may injure the spinal cord. Obviously, this could cause lasting damage. Thus, the major concern in managing an airway in the unconscious patient on the field is to protect the cervical spine. Any unconscious patient must be assumed to have cervical spine injury until proven otherwise. If the patient has an obvious head injury or laceration, the history indicates a force sustained by the neck, meaning that the trainer must be suspicious. This is a good example of the athletic trainer's first job: protecting the patient from any further injury.

How can one determine if the patient has a significant injury to the chest? Simply stated, the patient will have one or both of these symptoms: S/he will complain of pain in the chest or shortness of breath. Common statements are, "I have difficulty getting my breath; I have difficulty getting my wind; I can't breathe, I'm choking." Pain and shortness of breath are the cardinal symptoms of significant chest injury. On examination, the patient may have a contusion or bruising of the chest. Contusions anywhere on the body are not significant in and of themselves, but they are very significant in that they may hide underlying injuries. The chest may have a rib fracture, an injury to the underlying lung, or collapse of the lung. Contusions must be recognized for what might be underneath them and not for the bruises themselves.

Most sports-related injuries will be of a closed or internal nature. Closed injuries with external bleeding are unusual. The open wound or sucking wound to the chest (very rare in athletic competition) occurs after someone is shot in the chest. This chest injury has implications for a much more serious problem encountered in sports injuries: a tension pneumothorax, an injury discussed shortly.

Swelling of the face and neck indicates serious injury. After looking at the patient, the trainer should feel the patient's chest and try to detect where the injury might be. Obviously, the areas the patient says are hurting must be examined as well. Tenderness, direct tenderness, and crepitation (bones rubbing together) mean rib fractures. Extremely significant is tenderness over the sternum, for this may indicate an underlying injury to the heart. Sternal tenderness is extremely important to detect.

In examining a patient's chest, the physician uses a maneuver called "percussion." A good analogy to this technique is hanging a picture and trying to get the nail into a beam; one pounds along the wall with a hammer trying to detect where the studs are behind the wall. This is what the physician—and trainer—does on a patient's chest. The sounds to listen for with percussion are dullness or hyper-resonance, that is, a sound like a snare drum. Hyper-resonance means a collapsed lung, whereas a dull sound means the chest cavity is filling up with blood. These two sounds are extremely helpful in differentiating between injuries. The trainer should listen to the patient's lungs; if there are breath sounds on both sides, the lungs are not collapsed. If there are good breath sounds on one side and none on the other side, this is a significant finding. The trainer should be able to make that determination on the field or at least in the locker room.

During the normal process of inspiration, the diaphragm lowers and the chest wall symmetrically expands. The opposite occurs during expiration. The intrapleural pressure is the pressure in the potential space between the lining of the chest cavity called the parietal pleura and the pleura reflected over the lung itself, the visceral pleura. The space is usually obliterated and has a negative pressure relative to the atmosphere pressure. Therefore, if air is allowed into this pleural space, the lung will collapse.

Flail chest injury occurs with a direct blow to the chest, causing fractures to at least three adjacent ribs in at least two places. When the patient breathes in deeply, the affected portion of the chest wall collapses instead of expanding in the normal fashion. This compresses the normal lung tissue, which should be expanding and filling with air. During expiration, the opposite occurs. The chest wall goes out when it should be coming back in again. This is a see-saw motion in the ventilatory pattern that is not due so much to the compression of normal pulmonary tissue as it is to the associated injury to the underlying lung. A flail chest injury is extremely painful, and because of the pain, the patient will not take a deep breath. If the patient does not breathe deeply, s/he may develop cyanosis and become short of breath. The trainer should be able to determine this injury by observing paradoxical motion of the chest wall. This diagnosis does not come back from the X-ray department; it should be diagnosed by observing the patient's breathing, palpating crepitation, and noting shock.

The open pneumothorax is not common in sports injuries. The lung can collapse spontaneously in a young, healthy person, however, and if the patient does not have enough reserve in the opposite lung, s/he may arrest and possibly die. More commonly, the patient will ventilate the normal lung despite the other collapsed lung.

The most important chest injury discussed here is the tension pneumothorax. This condition can occur with only one fractured rib. The rib lacerates, or cuts into, the pleural lining and creates a flap. When the patient breathes in, air enters the pleural space, and when the patient breathes out, air cannot escape that pleural space. This causes increased pressure on the affected side. People who die on the roadside following an automobile accident commonly do so because of this chest injury. Tension pneumothorax is rapidly fatal unless it is recognized by the cyanosis and respiratory embarrassment. In this condition, the trachea, which is normally in the midline, is pushed away from the affected side because of the increased tension on the side of the collapsed lung. The diagnosis is made by percussing the patient's chest, which is hyperresonant and sounds like a drum. Also, there are no breath sounds on the affected side.

Athletic trainers must first consider this condition because if it is not promptly treated, the patient will go into shock.

The ironic aspect of tension pneumothorax is that the physician often decides the patient needs a definitive airway and so places an endotracheal tube into the throat and breathes for the patient by forced ventilation or positive pressure ventilation. Then suddenly the patient gets worse because positive pressure ventilation causes further collapse of the affected lung. This resultant shift of the structures to the opposite side causes angulation of the veins so that blood cannot get back to the heart, and if uncorrected, the patient dies. This is a serious pitfall in dealing with tension pneumothorax.

Another significant chest injury from an isolated rib fracture is a hemothorax, or bleeding into the chest cavity. This occurs in the thorax when an artery or vein is lacerated following rib fracture. Bleeding may be severe, filling the chest cavity with blood. The lung collapses and the patient suffers a serious loss of blood, becomes cyanotic, and has respiratory embarrassment. The percussion note will be dull, not hyperresonant as with a tension pneumothorax. Breath sounds will be absent or distant, for the compression of good lung tissue causes impaired ventilation, and the patient will go into shock. The importance of both tension pneumothorax and hemothorax cannot be understated; they are serious injuries that may follow modest trauma.

The last type of major chest injury is unusual but does occur following blunt trauma. The injury is known as "cardiac tamponade," in which the lining of the heart, the pericardial sac, fills up with blood. This is a common phenomenon following penetrating injuries to the chest such as gunshot wounds. In pericardial tamponade, the venous pressure is elevated and neck veins are distended. The neck veins also are distended with the tension pneumothorax for the same reason. Distended neck veins in the patient who has had significant chest trauma is a grave sign. Because the venous return to the heart is diminished, cardiac output drops, and the patient goes into shock.

Treatment of Chest Trauma

Again, the athletic trainer's first goal in dealing with patients who have chest trauma is to protect them from further injury. The second goal is to assess the patient and to try to determine whether the patient has one of the significant types of injuries discussed previously. The third goal is to provide emergency treatment until the patient can be evacuated to a medical facility.

In managing an injured patient, the single most important measure is establishing an airway. The best way to secure an airway is to observe the patient. If the patient is not coughing or if no sound is audible from his/her trachea, then the airway is obstructed. Airways may be established and protected by simple means, primarily by protecting the neck if the patient is unconscious. The heroic slash in the trachea should never be performed under any conditions other than in the controlled environs of a hospital, because a tracheotomy has a significant complication rate among the best of physicians under the best of circumstances.

Bleeding, if external, is not that serious a problem; it can be controlled by external pressure. Unfortunately, external bleeding is not the most common problem in the athlete. Internal bleeding is the more serious injury depending on its degree. If the patient is slowly bleeding, s/he will appear normal or only modestly injured at first and then may deteriorate later. Although brisk bleeding occurs and may require prompt operation, this is usually not the case.

If the patient is bleeding internally, his/her circulation must be re-established to prevent shock. Although athletic trainers are not expected to start intravenous solutions on the field, they should be able to detect the kind of assistance each patient needs. For example, with a patient who has a secured airway but seems to have respiratory distress, the trainer should consider flail chest, tension pneumothorax, hemothorax, and cardiac decompensation.

Other entities are important but not as common in athletic injuries (i.e., tracheal-esophageal rupture, subcutaneous emphysema, and traumatic rupture of the aorta). These injuries do not occur in sports injuries except with race-car drivers, because these are high-speed deceleration injuries that occur in highway accidents.

Thus, emergency treatment is *airway first*. Maneuvers to clear the airway will vary with the cause of the obstruction. With a suspected tension pneumothorax, it is best to convert it to an open pneumothorax by putting a needle into the pleural space. The patient will usually tolerate an open pneumothorax but not a tension pneumothorax. A big rush of air will come out through the needle after it is inserted and the patient will improve within seconds. If the diagnosis is uncertain, the needle should be placed on a syringe. If the plunger of the syringe comes out, the diagnosis is confirmed. This maneuver will not allow any air into the pleural space if the diagnosis is incorrect, although basically, athletic trainers must be confident of the diagnosis.

In flail chest, if the patient has multiple rib fractures, stabilizing that portion of the chest wall with sand bags or some type of compression is best. Also, laying the patient on the affected side will benefit the good side. The definitive treatment of a tension and open pneumothorax and hemothorax is insertion of a chest tube; this is performed in the emergency room after confirmation of the diagnosis.

Abdominal Trauma

Anything that injures the chest may also injure organs within the abdomen. The chest is separated by a sheath of muscle called the diaphragm. One of the organs at greatest risk in a chest injury is located under the left diaphragm: the spleen. Seventy percent of patients who rupture their spleen will have associated rib fractures along the lower left chest. Athletic trainers should suspect this when reviewing a patient's symptoms.

The abdomen consists of a number of organs and organ systems with isolated functions. There are hollow abdominal organs which act as organs of absorption, transit, or storage. An example would be the stomach, the small and large intestines, and the rectum. The gall bladder, bile ducts, ureter, and urinary bladder are conduits of storage. Solid abdominal organs regulate the normal biochemistry of the body and perform certain biochemical functions; examples are the liver, spleen, kidneys, and pancreas. There is a systematic approach to reviewing the abdomen in the injured athlete which should help the trainer discover what types of injuries a patient may have. It is best to think of the patient in terms of having hollow organs and solid organs because the risks differ. Abdominal injuries are classified as closed/blunt trauma (automobile accidents and sports injuries), or open (gunshot wounds and stabbings). We will discuss blunt abdominal trauma only.

Injuries to the hollow viscera will lead to contamination or chemical irritation of the peritoneal cavity. Bleeding is usually not a problem. If the contamination is allowed to persist, however, the patient will develop low blood pressure because s/he will lose large volumes of fluid into the abdominal cavity. A long-term risk is infection.

Injury to the solid viscera is a major problem because of the risk of bleeding. The patient may bleed into the peritoneal cavity, abdominal cavity, or retroperitoneal space and shock may result. The intestines receive their blood supply through the mesentery, which can also be injured. When the mesentery is injured, bleeding and shock can result. The other injury that may occur is direct injury to a blood vessel. If it is a major blood vessel, the patient can bleed to death before s/he can be saved.

The spleen is located in the left upper quadrant of the abdomen underneath the diaphragm, and right underneath the rib cage, and is the most commonly injured solid organ in the abdominal cavity. The reason this is so is because, despite its protected position, the spleen is a vascular organ with a thin, delicate capsule. The pulp of the spleen is easily injured. Injury occurs when there is a tear in the capsule and contusion of the underlying splenic pulp. The patient may bleed out from this area into the peritoneal cavity. Bleeding can be significant even from a small tear in the periphery of the spleen. If a laceration reaches the arterial supply, bleeding can be very severe and the patient will go rapidly into shock. This is a significant injury and one with which trainers must be concerned when dealing with abdominal trauma.

A liver laceration sustained in an automobile accident from a steering wheel is a common injury; this can also occur in athletic competition with injury or trauma to the right upper quadrant. The liver is located in the right upper quadrant underneath the diaphragm and protected by the ribs. The liver is unique in that it has two major blood supplies: an arterial blood supply and a supply from the portal vein. Bleeding from the liver may be very severe. In fact, if a patient has an injury to the liver that requires part of the liver to be removed, under the best of hands s/he will have a mortality rate of 50%. This is a significant type of injury, although a lesser degree of trauma to the liver can be patched with sutures or other techniques. Again, the diagnosis of a liver injury will be obvious if the bleeding is severe.

Injuries to the pancreas are especially treacherous. The pancreas produces a host of digestive enzymes that enter the intestinal tract at the duodenum and help digest food. If these enzymes are lost in the area of the pancreas, they digest the body, not the food. This is a major problem for the surgeon. In addition, pancreatic injuries are almost always accompanied by other organ injuries with significant bleeding. Often these injuries do not become apparent for 12 to 24 hours following injury.

The other organs apt to be injured in the abdominal cavity or the peritoneal cavity are hollow viscera, namely the intestines. The intestines are injured at two particular points. The first is injured by compression over bony prominences, and the second by shearing forces at the junction between what is fixed and what is mobile. Therefore, the intestine will be injured in the area of the duodenum, colon, and the junction between the duodenum and the small bowel, and the small bowel and the large bowel in the lower quadrant. Injury to the small bowel is the most common injury with seat belts. This patient suffers a major blunt injury to the abdomen and develops abdominal pain. The patient may not develop shock immediately, however, because s/he probably will not be bleeding excessively.

Behind the peritoneal cavity are the kidneys. The kidneys occupy a rather enviable position in the body because they are deep within the abdominal cavity surrounded by a thick layer of fat and protected by the lumbar spine and the posterior ribs. Right next to them is the vena cava and the aorta. The types of kidney injuries are basically subcapsular tears, which are of limited importance and probably cannot be picked up by the trainer (although the patient may have pain). A contusion which connects with the collecting system of the kidney or any type of injury that communicates with the collecting system—will be picked up because the patient will pass blood in his or her urine. This means the patient has an injury to the kidney or collecting system, automatically creating a greater risk for bleeding and infection. Mild injuries to the kidney are seldom recognized because they do not cause bleeding into the urine. In this condition, the patient may have slight pain or fever.

A major type of kidney injury is an injury to the blood vessels supplying the kidneys. This injury is not common in sports except in high-speed accidents, because it occurs following deceleration where the kidney is mobile and is torn off its pedicle. In this case, the patient bleeds from the aorta into the retroperitoneal space and may or may not make it to the hospital. If the patient does survive, s/he will need prompt surgical attention. Signs of injury to the kidney are local signs of external violence or overlying contusion and blood in the urine. The complications that may occur following kidney injury are loss of kidney function, infection, and high blood pressure, although the patient is at greatest risk from bleeding. Frequent monitoring of the vital signs and evacuating the patient to the hospital are the trainer's required responsibilities.

The urinary bladder and the urethra are the other important portions of the genito-urinary system that may be injured. The urinary bladder is protected by the bony pelvis but is vulnerable when distended. If the pelvis is not fractured, an empty bladder is almost impossible to injure. What are the signs of injury? First, injury to the lower abdomen, the pelvis, or the perineum could point toward injury to the bladder or urethra. Blood in the urine or the meatus suggests the patient either has a kidney, bladder, or urethra injury. Patients suffering these types of injuries will be in pain and may not be able to pass urine voluntarily, especially if the urethra is completely disrupted. Here again, the trainer must check the patient's vital signs and get him or her to the hospital.

Pelvic fractures, another possible injury from athletic accidents, are not common but are very serious if unstable. Therefore, the trainer must determine if the patient has an unstable pelvic fracture. The pelvis is shaped like a ring, protects the pelvic organs, and participates in weight bearing. The forces of weight bearing are transmitted through the lumbosacral spine and distributed across this pivotal link to the femurs. Disruption of the pelvis can lead to significant problems with weight bearing. The major problem in pelvic fracture is bleeding, for the blood vessels in the pelvis course along the bones in the pelvis. Breaking the pelvic bones, then, lacerates the vessels.

To diagnose a pelvic fracture or break in the ring, the trainer must examine the patient's pelvis with a compression-distraction maneuver. If the pelvic wings slide with compression, they are unstable. Patients also may have a pelvic fracture and not be unstable. Generally, these patients will not have serious problems unless they are bleeding, which is a significant cause of unwanted blood loss and is difficult to assess.

In summary, when taking care of patients with abdominal injuries, first place the patient in a comfortable position and record the vital signs, including the pulse rate and blood pressure. Observe the patient's behavior: Is the patient writhing in pain? Or is the patient lying there quietly, afraid to move? If the patient has any kind of irritation through the abdominal cavity, s/he will lie very still because every movement hurts. Reluctance to move or wincing when the stretcher is bumped is a sign of serious injury. Patients who are injured generally will have a full stomach, so trainers should expect vomiting. One of the major risks to injured patients is vomiting and aspirating the vomitus into the airway. Trainers must be alert and protect the patients by turning them on their sides so that they can vomit without danger.

Next, inspect the abdomen: Is it symmetrical? Are there overlying contusions? Is it swollen? Is it distended in one place? These are signs of injury. Listen to the abdomen; if the patient has no bowel sound, no gurgles, s/he has a significant injury. Percuss the abdomen just like the chest. If the patient reacts to the percussion, it suggests underlying inflammation of the peritoneal lining. This is a subtle but important diagnostic sign. Palpate, feel the patient's belly. If the patient is tender or stiffens the abdominal wall, s/he could have a serious injury.

Again, in treating an abdominal injury, protect the airway. The importance of the airway in the management of any patient with a musculoskeletal injury to the chest, abdomen, groin, urinary tract, or whatever cannot be overemphasized. Provide supplemental oxygen, especially if the patient is in shock, but do not administer anything by mouth because there is a risk of vomiting and aspirating. Also, do not give analgesics because the physician who eventually evaluates the patient does not want the individual to be under the effects of a drug. Monitor the patient's vital signs closely and then rapidly evacuate the patient to the hospital. Rapid, gentle transportation of the acutely injured patient is extremely important, for the body has a remarkable way of protecting itself from bleeding. It does this by a method known as "tamponade," a sort of external/internal pressure around the bleeding site. If the patient is moved randomly, the tamponade will become dislodged. Furthermore, sometimes the patient will bleed, then clot. The clot may become dislodged, causing the patient to bleed again, if the patient is moved too violently. Gentle transportation is extremely important in patients with pelvic as well as cervical fractures.

Diagnosis and Treatment of Shock

Gray, damp skin and low blood pressure are the classic signs of shock. Trainers want to be able to recognize shock when the patient has lost only 750 or 800cc of blood. The normal blood volume in an adult is about 5,000cc, so a patient who loses 15% of blood volume will be in serious trouble. Therefore, this condition must be recognized early, first by taking the patient's blood pressure. Pulse pressure is defined as the difference between the systolic blood pressure and the diastolic pressure. For instance, the normal blood pressure is 120/80. So, if a patient with a typical blood pressure of 120/80 has a blood pressure of 110/90 after injury, his or her pulse pressure has then been reduced by 50%. The trainer who doesn't keep this in mind will not be alarmed—which is a dangerous situation since the patient's blood pressure is dropping.

The early signs of shock are narrowed pulse pressure, mild hypotension, and elevated heart rate. The patient will also have an increased respiratory rate. (If the patient has been in competition, a relatively rapid respiratory rate will be expected anyway.) The patient also will be agitated, have a feeling of foreboding anxiety, and wonder what is happening.

There are three types of shock in the injured patient, especially in those with abdominal injury and bleeding.

1. Hypovolemic shock is the major type of shock with which trainers should be concerned. It is caused by inadequate fluid volume due to bleeding.

2. Cardiogenic shock means that the pump has failed and the heart will not fill. The major cause is a tension pneumothorax or pericardial tamponade.

3. Vasomotor shock is caused by vasodilation; spinal shock is an example.

Two new field techniques that deserve mention are the esophageal airway and antishock trousers. The esophageal airway is a relatively new device on the market and will be used in the field a lot more than it has ever been before. This device should only be used in a comatose patient, for otherwise, the patient may vomit. It can be put in quickly, within 30 seconds, inserted safely by anyone trained to use it, and can be inserted in the field. The patient does not have to wait to get to the operating room or the emergency room for a secure airway. This is its major advantage. The esophageal airway is a tube and a mask with a balloon on the end of the tube. The tube is placed blindly into the patient's mouth and is normally guided back into the esophagus; it should not go into the trachea. On the end of this tube is a balloon that can be blown up from the outside. This prevents air from getting into the stomach and any vomitus going from the stomach into the airway, another major advantage. The trainer then breathes the patient through the tube. Remember the air can be breathed by having this tight-fitting mask over the patient's face. This is the airway of choice, without question, if the status of the cervical spine is unknown, because the neck does not need to be manipulated to establish the airway.

This technique does have complications, however—for instance, the possibility of lacerating the esophagus or the pharynx. The tube could go into the trachea, which would be a disaster, but this is immediately recognizable. Also, in some patients the heart rate will drop with the tube in the esophagus. This is not common, but it does occur. Finally, if the patient has facial trauma and is bleeding, the esophageal airway should not be used.

The other field technique is known as "external counter pressure"—the "anti-shock trouser." This is another new item on the market that looks just like a big blood pressure cuff and is used for the treatment of shock. This device can be put on a patient in about 90 seconds by somebody who is skilled in its use. The "trousers" are either placed under the patient or the patient lifted onto the device. The patient is then wrapped in it. It has velcro straps which fit tightly around the patient's legs and abdomen and is blown up with a foot pump. This compresses the bleeding sites. This device is very effective. If the patient is bleeding in the abdomen, the pelvis, or the lower extremities, it will compress this area and prevent further blood loss. It also increases the circulating blood volume going to the central circulation—heart, brains, lungs—and re-establishes the circulation. The trousers save lives and prevent shock, but they interfere with the physical examination. They also prevent an assessment of the vascular status of the leg. This device should not be used in patients who have had heart failure.

Human beings are not as easily healed as they are hurt. (This is certainly true for sports injuries. It is true for all types of trauma.) Injuries to the chest and abdomen, although they have not been given the recognition they should in sports literature, are important, because prompt diagnosis and prompt and specific treatment can save an athlete's life.

The Rationale for Joint Mobilization

Sandy Burkhardt
West Virginia University

The purpose of this paper is to describe the various mechanisms responsible for contracture formation and how therapeutic exercise affects connective tissues. An appreciation of the fundamental principles of connective tissue remodeling is essential to a clear understanding of the rationale for peripheral joint mobilization.

Let's start with some relevant histology of connective tissue. Dense types of connective tissue are classified as regular or irregular. The regular fibers run in parallel directions and resist forces—the aponeuroses of the oblique muscles is an example—and tendons and ligaments also have parallel arrangements. Ligaments both permit and limit movement in certain directions. Irregular connective tissue is found in the fascia, dermis of the skin, joint capsules, and periosteum.

Consider a tendon inserting into bone at the level of the periosteum. Both kinds of connective tissue are present: dense, regular connective tissue with bundles of collagen fibers running in parallel array insert into the dense, irregular connective tissue of the periosteum. Remember that the external or fibrous layer of the periosteum merely extends over the joint capsule, becoming the external fibrous layer of the capsule. Because they are continuous, the structure of the external layer of the periosteum is very similar to that of the joint capsule: The difference is in the inner layers.

What are the functions of connective tissue? Support for attachment, which is mainly a function of collagen. Connective tissue also transports amino acids, oxygen, and waste products: The ground substance is the transport medium, and proteoglycans influence its structure. Storage is

Sandy Burkhardt, PhD, RPT, is director of physical therapy at West Virginia University in Morgantown, West Virginia.

another function, as well as protection against mechanical stress. Protection against pathogens is also necessary and the antigen-antibody reactions occur. The last function of connective tissue is repair, and this is the most important aspect to look at now, because our interest lies in the formation of contractures.

Let's review now the components of connective tissue cells-fibers and ground substance—realizing that this is a living, dynamic tissue in equilibrium, working as a functional matrix. Among the cells, fibroblasts are important. Because they synthesize proteoglycans for ground substance as well as collagen precursors, the fibroblasts actually control the amount of fibers formed and the type of ground substance present. The influence of these cells thus extends farther into the periphery.

Macrophages are phagocytic cells, important in inflammatory reactions and in the healing process. Other cells found in connective tissue include plasma cells with a cartwheel nucleus for antibody-antigen reactions, and mast cells which secrete heparin and histamine—the latter, of course, being responsible for the inflammatory signs seen in the joints.

The collagen fibers running through the tissue give it support, and ground substance is present throughout. The entire tissue receives nutritional factors and disposes of wastes by fluid transfer from the capillary beds: It is a living, dynamic structure.

Now, from connective tissue to the contracture. How is the basic histology of connective tissue related to some limitation of joint motion? In order to understand the flexibility within a healthy joint or a ligament, we must look at collagen synthesis.

Collagen is synthesized by a fibroblast, working in an environment which is the fibroblast's functioned matrix. The cell must adapt to this environment, whether it be normal or inflammatory.

In essence, the fibroblast is a minute factor. The administration, the genetic control, is in the nucleus which controls all the activity in the plant. The cell membrane is the boundary of the factory, and outside is the environment.

Raw materials, amino acids like proline and lysine, enter the environment in the fluid medium coming from the capillary beds. They pass into the cell to an area called the rough endoplasmic reticulum, which is an assembly line. It puts the amino acids together in chains and passes them along to the golgi apparatus. The processed materials—now called collagen precursors—are passed back out to the environment. The environment then begins to aggregate these collagen precursors (which are soluble) in a specific way, forming an insoluble form of collagen—the collagen fibril.

How does a collagen fibril get bigger? Many fibrils join together in parallel, linking by chemical bonds and thus making a collagen fiber, which is large in diameter. Individual fibers then join together, or hook onto larger collagen units, cross-linking chemically and giving structure to the tissue. The more stress there is on a tissue, the thicker the collagen units will become.

How important is collagen? Thirty-four percent of all bone is collagen. The matrix of cartilage consists of chondrocytes, ground substance, and collagen. There is collagen in connective tissue, in tendons, joint capsules, and ligaments. As orthopedic physical therapists, we must understand it.

In itself, collagen is not elastic. Collagen fibers must be strong because big muscles pull on tendons and ligaments, and because they have to be strong they cannot be elastic. Yet joint capsules do have tremendous flexibility, so where is that flexibility derived? It is derived from the weaving of the collagen fibers within the connective tissue structure. A good simile would be the Japanese "finger grabber" toys which you put two fingers into and pull, then cannot extricate your fingers. The pulling takes up the slack in the fabric, and the fibrous arrangement of that little toy then prevents you from pulling your fingers out.

Dense irregular connective tissue has a similar interweave of collagen fibers. The amount of flexibility is determined mainly by (a) the amount of collagen present and (b) the interspaces between the fibers. The greater the interspace between fibers, the greater the elasticity of the connective tissue structure. Another factor is the ability of these fibers to glide over one another. There has to be some lubricating mechanism, and this is a very important function of the ground substance. We know that ground substance binds with water and when it does so it becomes more viscous. It separates individual fibers and acts much like synovial fluid, preventing the individual fibers from chemically binding together at intersections.

These patterns or arrangements of collagen fibers are important to us, for when we have a contracture things will change. What happens when inflammation—caused by trauma or disuse—is imposed on the tissue structure? Connective tissue will react either by being destroyed or by forming scar tissue. These are the two major reactions. Remember what happens to the joints in rheumatoid arthritis? Collagenase, an enzyme, breaks down the collagen in the joint capsule, which becomes lax and prone to subluxation and dislocation.

The connective tissue repair process has three basic phases: substrate, fibroblastic, and maturation. The substrate phase is the inflammatory stage. There are a lot of dead cells, there is bleeding into the tissue, and neutrophils are present together with all kinds of broken down collagen. The joint or tissue is hot and painful.

Next comes the fibroblastic phase, with synthesis of new connective tissue. New fibers are laid down, blood vessels begin to grow into the injured area, and the tissue is restored to a near normal state. But any connective tissue then undergoes what is referred to as a maturation or remodeling phase, which continues perhaps for over a year, until finally the tissue is restored—hopefully to a stronger condition.

In this remodeling process, we are concerned about how the tissue is laid down and how we place physical forces on it. Young collagen synthesized in the fibroblastic phase has very small fibers. If we allow these fibers to remain immobilized, then the fibers will begin to get thicker and the elasticity of the tissue will decrease. As more chemical bonds are formed between collagen fibrils and the collagen fibers themselves, the contracture will become more severe. Contracture formation in the connective tissue involves the synthesis of more collagen, and the interspaces may decrease. Changes in the function of the ground substance occur so that it becomes thicker, allowing the possibility of chemical linking at intersection junctions. The whole process limits the elasticity of the connective tissue.

The joint capsule is the main structure we are going to mobilize. This capsule, remember, is dense, irregular connective tissue with two layers—an outer fibrous layer consisting mostly of collagen, and an inner synovial lining. There has to be an adequate arterial blood supply bringing raw materials, because the cells that make up the synovial membrane are both synthesizing cells and continually producing synovial fluid. A joint capsule is, therefore, a vascular tissue and this we have to keep in mind when we put a hard passive stretch on a tissue that has undergone contracture. It is possible to tear the vascular bed, resulting in bleeding into the joint periarticular tissue or even into the joint. This can increase the inflammatory state and prolong the rehabilitation time.

The joint capsule is also highly innervated with various types of nerve fibers. This joint is well-supplied with proprioceptive fibers and if there is inflammation within the joint, the painful response produces muscle spasm which limits the range of motion.

How is the mobility of a normal joint insured? The maintenance of periarticular connective tissue homeostasis has a lot to do with it. Whether active or passive, joint motion becomes a deforming force on the periarticular connective tissue. That force changes the environment of the matrix, setting off other changes. One cellular change involves the synthesis of collagen and proteoglycans in the ground substance. As these materials are released, the extracellular response includes (a) the aggregation of soluble collagen molecules, (b) the formation of chemical cross-links between collagen fibrils and fibers, (c) the alignment of collagen in the direction of stress, and (d) the formation of proteoglycan/water complexes in the matrix to increase the lubricating effect of the ground substance. This homeostatic mechanism thus maintains a strong, flexible joint capsule: Collagen maintains joint stability and also guides and limits motion in specific directions. This is really a whole fundamental feedback loop between stress and connective tissue involving both cellular and extracellular responses.

What happens when the joint becomes inflamed by trauma or disease? Clinical signs will be pain, muscle spasm, and limitation of the range of motion. Within the capsule the reaction to injury will be capsular destruction, laxity in terms of certain disease processes like rheumatoid arthritis, or a contracture will be formed within the connective tissue, limiting the range of motion.

What is the mechanism for contracture formation? The joint is immobilized by muscle spasm, by pain; there is decreased joint motion with decreased physical stress on the periarticular connective tissue; the cellular modulation is altered with decreased synthesis of collagen and proteoglycan. The major responses are the following: decreased water/proteoglycan complexes; the lubricating properties of the ground substance are lost; decreased water in the matrix lets the fibers come closer together and chemically cross-link, reducing elasticity and increasing fiber thickness. The response of the periarticular tissue is a joint contracture; loss of flexibility of the joint capsule, loss of joint play or accessory movement, and loss of active and/or passive range of motion.

What factors determine the degree of contracture? Certainly the extent of the trauma and the degree of inflammation: The greater the inflammatory response, the longer the repair process and rehabilitation time. The amount of pain and degree of muscle spasm are important—if the patient cannot move the joint, it is immobilized. Other factors include the amount of collagen that is laid down, the direction in which it is laid down, and the extent of connective tissue remodeling.

The connective tissue remodeling response is affected by other factors. Adequate protein intake is essential because amino acids are needed by synthesized collagen and many other protein structures. Vitamin C is necessary for collagen formation. Blood supply and oxygen tension must be adequate and the temperature has to be right for certain enzyme systems to work. Drugs, such as anti-inflammatory agents, can affect remodeling and the biomechanical stress of replacing the tissue.

Now we go back, within this framework, and ask, what we are doing to a periarticular contracture when we apply physical force through therapeutic exercise? There is a cellular modulation, a release of enzymes to break down old connective tissue. New collagen and proteoglycans are synthesized, causing connective tissue remodeling which includes (a) the realignment and lengthening of old fibers, (b) increased interfiber distance giving a little more flexibility to the tissues, (c) increased lubrication from the ground substance, and (d) the alignment of new collagen in relationship to stress. The end result is increased capsular elasticity, a restoration of joint play or accessory movement, a restoration of active and passive range of motion, a return of normal muscle power, and the resumption of normal life. We have, in essence, affected the whole individual by our contribution to connective tissue remodeling.

I have presented one mechanism that is involved in contracture formation. A second mechanism, involving myofibroblasts, interests researchers in hand surgery. Certain cells, called myofibroblasts, are beginning to predominate in contractures such as Dupuytrens contracture, Volkmanns ischemic contracture, and trigger finger. (Myo = muscle, fibroblast = synthesizing fiber.) These cells, which can not only synthesize things but also contract like muscle, are being found in high levels in these contractures.

What is a contracture by a myofibroblast? A pulling together of adjacent collagen fibers, an active process which decreases the flexibility of the tissue. We know that this function is important because these cells are found in skin wound repair, helping to pull the ends together.

How does this myofibroblast process seem to work? A normal fibroblast has a nucleus, mitochondria, rough endoplasmic reticulum, and the golgi apparatus. Smooth muscle cells, in contrast, have as their most characteristic feature the presence of actin and myocin filaments within the cytoplasm. These give muscle cells their contractile power. There are no actin and myocin filaments in normal fibroblasts.

But what happens if we change the environment of a fibroblast—put it into an inflammatory state and change its functional matrix? It seems to change its function, develops actin and myocin filaments in its cytoplasm and acquires the ability to both contract and relax. Various pharmacological agents, such as serotonin, bradykinin, and prostaglandin, will make these cells contract in culture. Other pharmacological agents, including prostaglandin, act as relaxing agents or inhibitors. So, in myofibroblastic-type contractures, there is now some possibility of developing a pharmacologic agent which can alter the response of the cell.

This work on myofibroblastic contractures is still experimental and primarily of interest to plastic surgery researchers. It is, however, a research approach of which we should be aware.

Implications of Tissue Healing to Treatment

John Spiker
West Virginia University

This paper will discuss the physiological process involved in an acute injury and the appropriate steps to be taken in immediate care treatment. First, what exactly is an injury? What happens to the body when an injury occurs? Tissue is injured when a force is greater than the tissues receiving it can withstand, and the degree of injury is determined by the amount of force. Injuries are classified as mild, moderate, and severe. The severe injury results in rupturing of tissue, thus producing complete laxity. The moderate injury results in some tearing and laxity, and the mild—being the most common—results in no significant disruption or laxity.

The local inflammatory reaction to soft tissue injury is important for the athletic trainer to understand. The first thing to occur is a separation in the tissue; the tissue is torn. One should consider this like a tear, such as when we accidentally cut ourselves; the same reaction occurs at a cellular level. When cells are torn apart, they lose their nutrition, resulting in cell death. With cell death, the enzyme necrosin is released. Then, histamine is released from the histiocytes, which are commonly called mast cells. Heparin is thought to be released as well, but less is known about the release of heparin than about histamine or necrosin. Heparin is an anticoagulant, but in this case, it does not necessarily work to the patient's advantage.

The amount of local inflammatory response is proportional to the tissue injury and death. This secondary insult, which can often be eliminated with immediate treatment, often occurs because of lack of appropriate immediate care. Inflammation is magnified because necrosin,

John Spiker, MS, RPT, ATC, is NATA curriculum director at West Virginia University in Morgantown, West Virginia.

released during cell death, produces a chemotoxic effect in the local area. The phagocytic cells then combine with the platelets and the fibrinogens, walling off and separating the injured area; this results in decreased nutrition to that area. We want to minimize the intracellular and extracellular fluid because it separates the damaged tissue more than the original trauma. Healing by what could have been first intention may no longer be possible, and second or third intention healing is then required. Thus, delaying treatment of an injury can greatly increase the time it takes an injury to heal, and this is obviously something the trainer is trying to avoid.

Another complication with injuries is hemorrhage. Histamine, released from the histiocyte and the mast cells, increases capillary permeability. This allows the various fluids to flow easily across the membranes. With the release of histamine, the blood would not traverse quite as easily and would develop a clot more easily and quickly. The anticoagulant effect of heparin leads to more complications—increased hemorrhage, separation of tissue, and edema—and thus more irritation.

Coupled with injury is pain. Much is yet to be learned about pain; we do not know what makes one person perceive pain more or differently than others, for example. It is realized, however, that pain dictates much to both the patient and the trainer. Pain is the governing force of all our treatments. When pain exists, the pain-spasm-pain cycle becomes apparent. This cycle produces decreased nutrition, resulting in less than optimal gaseous exchange between the tissues. Because of this, patients are unable to produce quality muscular contraction, delaying rehabilitation. Another undesirable effect of the pain-spasm-pain cycle is ischemia. This, too, reduces nutrition to the injured area, which in turn stimulates more spasm. Therefore, cells that were not before injured, die. If treatment does not break into the cycle, the pain-spasm-pain cycle and other associated effects continue.

Rehabilitation must begin when the injury is evaluated, and as just discussed, immediate care is critical in rehabilitation. Ice, compression, elevation, and immobilization are common to athletic trainers, and there are distinct physiological reasons for administering this sequence. The pain-injury cycle is disrupted by administering ice. The first result of ice is an anesthetic effect, which is important because anesthesia reduces spasm. The application of ice alone is valuable as an immediate care device because of its anesthetic effect. Also, ice decreases clotting time because its application increases the viscosity of the fluids. The quicker clotting effect allows less hemorrhage in the tissue, helping to reduce the amount of separation of the tissue. A critically important effect of ice is decreased cell metabolism. This has a great effect on the cells surrounding the injured area. When ice is administered to the local area, the cells surrounding the injury require fewer nutrients than normal because they are not working as hard. The application of ice decreases cell metabolism, in effect putting them into a state of hibernation. Until the repair process begins, hibernation is necessary, for as stated previously, an injured area receives fewer nutrients than normal. Without this decreased metabolism, the cells would require oxygen, which is simply not available from an impaired blood supply, and would die. In short, an injury 1 centimeter in circumference may become 3 without the immediate application of ice.

Next, why is compression important? Compression, besides being a mechanical deterrent to swelling, most likely is concerned with proprioception. Very little is known about proprioception. It is known that with a mild sprain, an elastic wrap on that injury renders little support. The pressure, however, makes it feel better. Why? In theory, it feels better because the proprioceptors are excited secondary to the pressure. Perhaps the proprioceptors are competing for and with the pain fibers. We do know that compression deters swelling because it keeps fluid out of the injured area.

Compression is the aspect of immediate care that is the most difficult to administer. Few people, other than athletic trainers, try to put on any kind of pressure, or even know how to put on pressure in the form of taping or wrapping after an injury. Accentuating the pressure at the injury site is critical. For example, placing a felt horseshoe around a sprained ankle is effective in reducing swelling. Pressure accentuated over the injured area will prevent swelling from separating those torn endings and produce healing by first intention. Accentuating the pressure is effective when one can localize the injury, such as with a simple ankle sprain. A relatively simple compression technique is using cold sponges for pressure. These sponges are kept in ice water and used to accentuate pressure in an area after injury. These work well on irregular surfaces such as the medial retinaculum of the knee following a subluxed or dislocated patella. The acromioclavicular area is also a good location for the application of cold sponges, for an ice bag rarely puts adequate pressure there.

Elevation, the third factor in the sequence, is used to limit fluid pooling and to encourage venous return. Failure to elevate an injury will lead to separation of tissues. Elevation should be extreme in a healthy, young athlete. For example, having an athlete lie supine with the sprained ankle resting high on the wall is a good technique. A more aggressive approach with immediate care would often prove valuable.

Immobilization is dependent upon the trainer's and physician's philosophy. Primarily, immobilization minimizes the additional stress on the torn tissue. Early immobilization is good, aggressive care. An athlete on crutches 1 day may eliminate 2 or 3 days of limping.

All immediate care treatments are attempts to create an optimal en-

vironment for healing. The four-step sequence—ice, compression, elevation, and immobilization—produces faster and less painful healing.
Failure to use this sequence can only make an injury even more traumatic
and difficult to treat.

Transcutaneous Electrical Nerve Stimulation: Research Update

Florene Carnicelli Johns
Physiotherapy Associates

This is truly an exciting time to be involved in the treatment of acute and chronic pain. Countless articles are being written and research is being performed in the area of nonsurgical and nonchemical means for influencing the body's threshold for pain. Today, transcutaneous electrical nerve stimulation (TENS) is being widely used for this purpose. Application of this treatment can be confusing, however, because determining such things as selection of the proper intensity, frequency, and duration of doses, and proper electrode placement may be difficult.

Until recently, Melzack and Wall's (1965) Gate-Control Theory of pain was widely used to explain how the intensity of noxious input could be reduced. According to their theory, specific or nondiscrete nociceptive (painful) impulses are conveyed to the spinal cord over small-diameter, afferent fibers to the substantia gelatinosa in the cord before transmitting them to the posterolateral horn. Input from pressoreceptors or mechanoreceptors travel along more rapidly conducting, large diameter A fibers. If the impulses are greater over the small diameter fiber groups, they will inhibit the substantia gelatinosa inhibitory interneurons. This opens the synaptic "gate," intensifying the pain. If these impulses are blocked at the substantia gelatinosa by stimulation of the large-diameter afferent fibers, however, then the inhibitory substantia gelatinosa cells will be inhibited. The gate closes and the pain is reduced (Melzack & Wall, 1965).

Also, cerebral cortical mechanisms responsible for sensory-discriminatory, motivation-affect, and cognition processes may relay impulses to the substantia gelatinosa that can close the gate. This supports

Florene Carnicelli Johns, RPT, is a physical therapist at Physiotherapy Associates in Nashville, Tennessee.

the importance of behavior therapy, which employs such techniques as relaxation, biofeedback, and psychotherapy.

The Gate-Control Theory recently has been criticized because results from studies using experimentally induced nociceptive applications in humans have not corroborated the theory as an explanation for the action of TENS in changing pain thresholds. There is little question that TENS can produce an effect on pain perception, for its clinical use has been successful, but specific mechanisms are being investigated. The discovery that the brain possesses an intrinsic endorphin-mediated analgesia system that can be activated by opiates or electrical stimulation and that operates through an efferent or descending pathway originating in the midbrain to suppress pain-transmission neurons has offered another possible explanation for the effects of TENS (Fields & Basbaum, 1978). Terenius (1978), at the University of Uppsala, Sweden, developed a means of monitoring endorphin concentrations in the human cerebrospinal fluid.

Andersson (1979) recently demonstrated that low frequency, intense stimulation increases the pain threshold in animals and humans. He determined that high-intensity electrical stimulation causing phasic muscle contraction is required to influence low and high threshold afferents both directly and via receptors. Muscle contractions activate muscle afferents as well as skin and joint afferents due to the movements occurring from stimulation. This type of stimulation has a long induction time of 15 to 20 minutes and a long-lasting aftereffect. In low treatment stimulation, the pain perception is altered not only in the areas stimulated, but also beyond these areas.

In contrast, high-frequency (50-100 Hz) stimulation at any intensity does not raise the pain threshold in humans, although it does inhibit certain painful conditions (see Table 1). This suggests the possibility that different neuronal mechanisms may be involved in high- and low-frequency stimulation. The patient receiving high-frequency stimulation experiences no phasic muscle contractions, although a mild tonic contraction may occur in muscles close to the electrodes. Pain perception is altered only in the segments stimulated.

SjoLund and Ericksson (1979) measured concentrations of endorphin fractions in the cerebrospinal fluid of patients before and after acupuncture-like, low-frequency TENS using surface electrodes. An increase of endorphin fraction I concentration was noted in lumbar cerebrospinal fluid of patients receiving low-frequency stimulation. In other experiments, no increase was noted with conventional high-frequency TENS.

Patients stimulated with low-frequency TENS and with conventional high-frequency TENS both experienced pain relief. The endorphin antagonist naloxone hydrochloride was then used and the patients receiving

Table 1

**Comparison of TENS (Above 10 Hz) and
Acupuncture (Electrical or Manual Below 10 Hz)**

	TENS	Acupuncture
Stimulation parameters		
Frequency	40-100 Hz	1-4 Hz
Intensity	Low	High
Electrodes	Surface (needles)	Surface or needles
Stimulation	Electrical	Electrical or manual
Discharge in afferents	Continuous in low-threshold afferents from skin and possibly muscles	Continuous or bursts in low- and high-threshold afferents mainly in muscles
Sensations	Tingling, vibration	Teh Chi, close to pain, beating
Analgesia		
Induction time	Short	Long
Distribution	Segmental	Segmental and nonsegmental
Duration	Individual	Individual
Aftereffect	Individual	Long-lasting
Pain-threshold effect	Transient	Long-lasting

Adapted from "Pain Control by Sensory Stimulation" by S.A. Andersson. In *Advances in Pain Research and Therapy* (Vol. 3). New York: Raven Press, 1979.

low-frequency TENS experienced inhibition of pain relief, whereas none of the patients receiving high-frequency TENS did so. This supports the idea that endorphins are involved in the pain-relieving mechanisms of low-frequency, high-intensity TENS (SjoLund & Ericksson, 1979).

Today, a great deal of controversy exists over the pulse width. Most TENS units provide pulse widths ranging from 40 to 500 u sec; some units have preset pulse widths. Lampe (1978) suggests a setting of 130 u sec. He demonstrates that increasing the width adjustment increases the strength of the stimulus perceived but alters the wave-form.

Duration of treatment also varies. Usually high-frequency TENS is applied for longer periods than the low-frequency type used over acupuncture points. This is an individual decision depending on the patient's response. I usually apply TENS at low frequency (3 Hz) for 20-30 minutes, with good results in reduction of chronic pain.

Electrode Placement

Anatomical and physiological principles should be applied when selecting stimulation sites. A sound knowledge of etiology, location, and character of pain is essential. Pain can be experienced locally. It can be referred from trigger points in muscles, ligaments, and viscera and can radiate along nerve pathways. Proper evaluation of the patient is therefore critical to achieving success with TENS.

The electrodes may be placed over local pain areas, dermatomes, peripheral nerves, acupuncture points, trigger points, or spinal cord segments. At least a four-electrode dual channel system usually is preferred to one having fewer electrodes because it enables the clinician to treat several points at once.

Units differ greatly in specifications. Using one particular unit may mean the difference between success and failure, so it is wise to have more than one type available in a setting.

Dermatomes can be stimulated in several ways. A random site can be selected but even better, motor points, muscular trigger points, or acupuncture points lying within the dermatome may be used. Peripheral nerves can be stimulated at a superficial point, but the electrodes must be placed proximal to a peripheral nerve lesion or the result may be a block in the input and in increased pain (Long, 1973). Spinal cord segments can be stimulated beside the vertebrae or between the spinous processes to reduce localized vertebrae column pain.

I most frequently apply TENS to acupuncture points, which makes it important to acquire acupuncture charts. Several courses are being offered over the country in different approaches to the application of TENS. An area known as applied kinesiology has recently been expanded in which acupuncture points and meridians are being tested for involvement, thereby aiding in selection of treatment points. This is an interesting approach and research is being attempted to support its use. There are also electrical units being used to test acupuncture points. Several courses are being offered over the country on different approaches to their application, and athletic trainers would find it valuable to study and apply the principles presented in their setting.

References

The Academy of Traditional Chinese Medicine: An outline of Chinese acupuncture. Peking: Foreign Languages Press, 1975.

ANDERSSON, S.A. Pain control by sensory stimulation. In Advances in pain research and therapy (Vol. 3). New York: Raven Press, 1979.

FIELDS, H.L., & Basbaum, A.I. Efferent control of pain-transmission neurons. Second World Congress on Pain, 1978, 1, 166 (Pain Abstracts).

LAMPE, G.N. Introduction to the use of transcutaneous electrical nerve stimulation devices. *Physical Therapy*, 1978, **58**, 1450-1454.

LONG, D.M. Electrical stimulation for relief of pain from chronic nerve injury. *Journal of Neurosurgery*, 1973, **39**, 719-722.

MATSUMOTO, T. *Acupuncture for physicians.* Springfield, IL: Charles C. Thomas, 1974.

MELZACK, R., & Wall, P.D. Pain mechanisms: A new theory. *Science*, 1965, **150**, 971-979.

SJOLUND, B.H., & Ericksson, M.B.E. Endorphins and analgesia produced by peripheral conditioning stimulation. In *Advances in pain research and therapy* (Vol. 3). New York: Raven Press, 1979.

TERENIUS, L. Endorphin mechanisms in chronic pain. *Second World Congress on Pain* (Vol. 1), 1978 (Pain Abstracts).

The Use of Drugs in Sports

Steven Roy
Center for Sports Medicine & Running Injuries of Eugene

Athletic trainers should be keenly aware of indications, dosage, and side effects of medications commonly used in the training room setting, as well as what these medications look like. An athlete frequently will have questions about his or her medication and will ask the trainer about them. Trainers must also recognize when to refer athletes for specific medications; they should particularly be aware of anti-inflammatory medication, which should be commenced soon after the injury to be effective.

Anti-inflammatory Agents

Anti-inflammatory agents are very commonly used in athletics and the athletic trainer should be fully acquainted with their indications, precautions, contraindications, and side effects.

Aspirin

Aspirin is a useful anti-inflammatory when used in high doses (over eight tablets per day) as well as a useful analgesic. In such high doses, however, it may cause gastric irritation or tinnitus. The gastric irritation may be reduced by taking the aspirin with food, using a combination of aspirin with an antacid (such as Ascriptin with Maalox) or an enteric-coated aspirin. Aspirin may also be taken prophylactically before participation when a condition such as "tennis elbow" or patellar tendinitis exists. Two or three aspirin tablets may be taken ½-1 hour before par-

---

Steven Roy, MD, is a physician and director of the Center for Sports Medicine & Running Injuries of Eugene in Eugene, Oregon.

ticipating in an athletic event.

Some investigators have stated that aspirin may help stimulate regeneration of articular cartilage, particularly in those who have chondromalacia of the patella. This is still a controversial issue, however. In some rare instances, a hypersensitivity may develop, manifested by the onset of bronchospasm and asthma.

It should be noted that two commonly used analgesics do not have anti-inflammatory properties: acetaminophen (Tylenol) and propoxyphene (Darvon). In addition, Darvon has been shown to cause serious problems and even death when taken in overdosage, particularly in combination with alcohol.

The Arylalkanoic Derivatives

These derivatives include the anti-inflammatories Motrin, Nalfon, Naprosyn, and Tolectin. Of these, Motrin is probably the most commonly used in athletics, although it should be realized that none has been approved specifically for use in athletic injuries by the FDA.

Motrin has good analgesic and anti-inflammatory properties that are similar to aspirin, and it can be used as a substitute for aspirin when aspirin cannot be tolerated in high doses. Motrin appears to be relatively safe, although some instances of gastrointestinal upsets have been noted. If gastrointestinal side effects do occur, they may be relieved to some extent by combining the drug with meals, milk, or antacids. Occasionally, dizziness or headache may occur as well as tinnitus, but on the whole, side effects are relatively infrequent. The dose most commonly used is 800 mg three times a day.

The other anti-inflammatories mentioned have a similar structure to Motrin, but all suffer from some side effects without demonstrating a marked superiority in action. Nalfon sometimes causes drowsiness, Naprosyn and Tolectin may cause gastrointestinal irritation and bleeding.

Indocin is not commonly used today in athletic circles, but Clinoril, which is similar in structure, is currently in favor. Although Clinoril may be more powerful than Indocin, it does have the side effects of gastrointestinal upsets, and occasionally, bleeding. Dizziness, headache, tinnitus, and edema have also been reported. The usual dose is 150 mg to 200 mg twice a day with food, and it is administered for up to 14 days at a time. Clinoril is probably a bit more powerful than Motrin and the other such drugs but less powerful in its anti-inflammatory action than Butazolidin or Tandearil.

Butazolidin and Tandearil

These two drugs, which have been on the market for many years, are similar in structure as well as in action and side effects. They are well known to be potentially hazardous drugs and should be used with the utmost discretion. But they can be beneficial if their use and side effects are well understood, however.

The side effects of these two drugs are mostly related to the gastrointestinal tract: dyspepsia, nausea, and occasionally intestinal bleeding from activation of a peptic ulcer. Butazolidin alka is a buffered form of Butazolidin and may produce slightly less gastric irritation than plain Butazolidin. Tandearil has a slightly lower incidence of gastrointestinal side effects, but it is not immune from producing such problems. Edema may also occur, particularly in the premenstrual female. The most significant and potentially lethal side effects relate to the depression of blood-forming tissues, resulting in agranulocytosis or aplastic anemia. Depression of the blood-forming tissues occurs most commonly because of the length of time that the drug has been used, but sometimes the occurrence of these side effects may result from a sensitivity to the drug after only a brief exposure. These are the side effects that have brought Butazolidin and Tandearil into ill repute.

Because of these serious side effects, certain precautions should be followed:

1. The athlete should not be given Butazolidin or Tandearil if s/he has a history of dyspepsia, a peptic ulcer, or gastric bleeding.

2. The usual course in the athlete should be limited to from 3 to 7 days, with 2 weeks being the outside maximum. The drugs should be monitored so that during a season they are not used for more than a total of about 3 weeks.

3. They should always be taken at the end of a meal with milk or similar antacid. They should not be taken with black coffee or alcohol, or on an empty stomach.

4. If more than two courses of the anti-inflammatory agent are given during a season, a full blood count should be performed and the athlete then monitored at regular intervals.

Dosage Schedule—A number of dosage schedules might be used with the athlete. The most common is to take 200 mg three times a day for about 3 days, then reduce the dosage to 100 mg three times a day for another 2 or 3 days. Alternatively, they may be used in the schedule of decreasing doses starting at 800 mg a day for the first day, decreasing to 600 mg a day the second day, 500 mg the third and fourth days, 400 mg the fifth and sixth days, and 300 mg on the seventh day.

Corticosteroids

Because corticosteroids are frequently used in athletics, their use needs to be carefully understood so that they are not abused. The corticosteroids are powerful anti-inflammatory agents and therefore popular. They have a number of serious side effects, however, which limits their use. These include the suppression of the adrenal gland, the precipitation of diabetes, the development of osteoporosis, the development of glaucoma, and mental and psychological changes. A number of other side effects may also occur if the drug is used for a long period of time. Locally, they may reduce the tensile strength of tendons and ligaments.

Corticosteroids may be very helpful in some athletic injuries, but they definitely should not be injected into certain anatomical areas because of the side effects that can easily occur. These are as follows:

1. Corticosteroids should not be injected into a tendon or a ligament, for that structure will tend to be weakened for at least 2 to 6 weeks. If the athletic activity is continued after such an injection, the weakened tendon or ligament may undergo complete rupture, particularly if the symptoms are masked by the cortisone.

2. Intra-articular degeneration and arthritis may develop if cortisone is injected into the knee joint, particularly if injected on a number of occasions.

Corticosteroids may be used in some areas, however, as long as the injury is accurately diagnosed and the drugs are used with discretion. For example, they are very useful in contusions to the distal end of the clavicle ("shoulder pointer") or to the iliac crest ("hip pointer"). They may also be used in some conditions of the foot, particularly Morton's neuroma between the metatarsal heads, as well as occasionally under a tendon sheath, such as a tenosynovitis of the thumb extensor tendons or the extensor tendons of the foot. Corticosteroids may, on occasion, be injected for some specific conditions around the ankle, but this is a controversial subject. Usually, cortisone is injected in combination with a local anesthetic agent such as "Xylocaine" or "Marcaine." In some cases, hyaluronidase ("Wydase"), a spreading agent, may also be included.

Oral Corticosteroids

Oral corticosteroids are seldom used in athletic medicine because of the dangers of systemic side effects. If they are prescribed, they should be used for less than 5 consecutive days because adrenal suppression will be less likely to develop with a short course.

Muscle Relaxants

These agents have a limited place in the treatment of athletic injuries. They seem to have a poor to moderate effect in relieving muscle spasm when used in the recommended dosage and, if used in higher dosage, have a marked sedative effect which restricts their potential use in the active individual. In a hospital setting probably the most useful of the muscle relaxants is Valium, but using such a drug frequently with an athlete has obvious problems.

Fluori-methane, when used by the local spray and stretch technique, may be very effective in providing temporary or even long-term relief of local muscle spasm and is a much more applicable form of therapy in a training room setting. Techniques in the use of Fluori-methane in trigger points have been discussed by Mennell and Travell.

Analgesics

The mildest analgesic possible should be used with the athlete, particularly in sports such as football, where repeated and constant "hurts" are being experienced. Treating athletes with an analgesic containing codeine may precipitate a problem with abuse and addiction. A compound containing codeine should be used only in selected cases. Also, a note should be made in the athlete's file that the compound was described on a particular day, and for the length of time it was used, so that one may see at a glance how many times during a particular season a particular analgesic has been administered. In most cases, the use of aspirin or Motrin is sufficient analgesic medication.

Cold Medications

Pseudoephedrine ("Sudafed")

This vasoconstrictor is very useful for dealing with the symptoms of an upper respiratory infection and rhinitis in an athlete. The advantage for athletes is that this drug does not cause drowsiness, which is the main problem with most "cold medications" containing an antihistamine. It does have some side effects, however, including stimulation, which may produce hyperactivity and insomnia in some sensitive athletes, or when too high a dosage is taken. Some reports of hypertension following administration of "Sudafed" have also been received.

Nose Drops

Nose drops appear to be fairly innocent drugs but should be used with a great deal of caution, particularly with athletes. If used persistently, nose drops can cause a reaction in which the mucosa first constricts but then rapidly swells in a rebound effect a short while later. Further administration of drops will again relieve the constriction with a resultant further rebound phenomenon. This "addiction" may occur in anyone, but particularly those unaware of its potential.

If nose drops are prescribed, the minimum amount should be prescribed for the shortest period possible. The athlete should be warned against overdosage and told to stop administering the drops as soon as the nasal obstruction is relieved.

Antibiotics

The most common need for antibiotics with athletes are (a) strep throat, (b) skin infections. Strep throat is usually treated with oral penicillin in the form of Pen-Vee-K for a total of 10 days. Skin infections are usually staphylococcal in origin and may be treated with erythromycin. If the bacteria are resistant, oral penicillin in the form of cloxicillin or dicloxicillin can be used. In addition, local antibiotic ointment in the form of Polysporin or Neosporin should be applied. The more serious infections may be treated with a broader spectrum antibiotic as indicated (such as Keflex).

Antidiarrheal Agents

Lomotil

Lomotil is an antidiarrheal agent that contains a morphine-like derivative as its main constituent together with atropine. It is usually very effective in the nonspecific gastrointestinal upset that plagues many traveling athletes. Because of the atropine content, however, some athletes might have difficulty in focusing accurately after taking Lomotil and may also complain of a dry mouth. The usual dosage is two tablets four times a day in the adult; the use in children has to be carefully prescribed because serious side effects may occur.

Medications Suitable for Constipation

Athletes might suffer from constipation particularly when traveling through time zone changes. "Metamucil," which causes very little irritation or cramping, is a useful agent. The "Fleet" enema may be used for the acutely desperate athlete.

.

Antifungal Agents

Although commonly used preparations such as Tinactin and Desenex are undoubtedly useful, probably the most effective topical preparation is Lotrimin, which not only acts as an antifungal but also inhibits the growth of yeasts (Candida albicans) as well as M. furfur, the agent that causes tinea versicolor. It may be used either as a cream or as a solution and should be applied at least twice a day and for approximately a week after the symptoms disappear.

Medication for Exercise-induced Asthma

An athlete who has exercise-induced asthma will not benefit from the use of cortisone, unlike the person with long-standing chronic asthma. Probably the two best forms of medication for exercise-induced asthma are (a) the preventative use of cromolyn sodium just before the exercise. This may be repeated at half-hour intervals if necessary (twice or three times), or (b) Brethine tablets, preferably half an hour before the event.

Aphthous Ulcers

These frequently annoying mouth ulcers may be controlled to some extent with tetracycline powder from a capsule of tetracycline, dissolved in water and swilled around the mouth for a few minutes three or four times a day.

Anabolic Steroids

The subject of anabolic steroids immediately elicits a wide variety of emotions among athletes, coaches, trainers, and sports medicine physicians. There seems to be a clearly divided line between opposing sides, the coaches and athletes on one side claiming that anabolic steroids help strength and athletic performance, while most physicians counter that the drugs have no benefit and are banned to protect athletes from side effects. No report in the literature reviewed, however, has revealed significant side effects in athletes taking anabolic steroids. Shephard et al. studied six body builders taking Dianabol in intermittent courses for a year or more; the body builders did not suffer from any subjective disturbance, but had relatively low testosterone and luteinizing hormone levels. Abnormal liver function tests were seen in three of the six subjects, and one had mild diabetes with high-serum cholesterol, triglycerides, and uric acid. It is difficult to know what this actually means, as these could have been chance findings unrelated to the administration of steroids.

One of the best reviews on anabolic steroids is by Ryan.[1] In reviewing the world literature, Ryan discussed 30 laboratory or clinical studies involving the experimental use of anabolic steriods in males. His careful review of all of these reports leads to an inescapable conclusion that no substantial evidence supports the claims that the use of anabolic steroids by athletes in conjunction with progressive resistance training affords a greater increase in muscle bulk and greater strength. On the contrary, a substantial body of evidence, even under close scrutiny, indicates that anabolic steroids given orally or parenterally do not contribute significantly to gains in muscle size and strength in healthy, young males.

The trainer should be aware of the paucity of well-documented advantages to taking anabolic steroids and therefore should refrain from encouraging their use. He or she should also be aware of the potential side effects in terms of testosterone depression, hepatic dysfunction, premature closure of the epiphyses in a growing teenager, as well as masculinization of the female athlete. Trainers should attempt to educate athletes about the physical dangers but should not be shy about dealing with the ethical considerations of the use of drugs in sports.

Amphetamines

Amphetamines were undoubtedly the curse of the sports world during the sixties and early seventies, until eventually the tremendous dangers of these drugs were sufficiently publicized. They were implicated in the deaths of a number of long-distance cyclists as well as the death of a French basketball player in the 1968 Olympic Games in Mexico City. In 1972, a report noted that 70 athletes died from amphetamines and other doping agents in the sixties.

The main danger of amphetamines appears to be their ability to cause euphoria and increase the threshold for pain. This then allows a highly motivated individual to work at maximum capacity for a longer period of time than normally would be possible, thereby using more energy from anaerobic sources. This removal of the normal inhibitions of fatigue allows an athlete to literally work him or herself to death, particularly when in a hot environment. A disturbance in temperature regulation also may occur; this is thought to have caused the death of several European cyclists which were attributed to heat stroke. The mechanism of this disturbance in temperature regulation is thought to be due to constriction of cutaneous arterials, thereby decreasing heat

[1]Ryan, A.J. In G.V.R. Born et al., (Eds.), *Handbook of Experimental Pharmacology* (Vol. 43). Berlin-Heidelberg: Springer-Verlag, 1976.

elimination. The other frightening danger of amphetamines is their ability to cause severe addiction from which the athlete may have great difficulty in withdrawing. Amphetamines should be condemned in the strongest terms and should never be considered for use by athletes under any circumstances.

Portions of this presentation appear in Steven P. Roy, *Sports Medicine for the Athletic Trainer*, published by Prentice-Hall, Englewood Cliffs, NJ.

PART THREE

PREVENTING ATHLETIC INJURIES THROUGH HEALTH AND FITNESS

Physiological Effects of Strength Training and Various Strength Training Devices

Jack H. Wilmore
University of Arizona

Strength training is an exciting area, one about which we still know little. This paper will share the very limited knowledge we do have about strength training. First, I would like to briefly present our current knowledge in the area of muscle physiology as a basic foundation for the discussion on the muscle during strength training programs.

The muscle is composed of many small muscle fibers, which are further broken down into myofibrils consisting of a number of repetitive units. One repetitive unit is referred to as a sarcomere, and the sarcomere is the basic contractile mechanism of the muscle. The basic cell of the muscle is the muscle fiber, which is multinucleated.

A muscle fiber begins its contraction as the individual myofibrils shorten. The action potential travels down the motor nerve to the motor endplate. It is spread along the length of the fiber and enters the fiber through the T-tubule pores. The T-tubules continue into the sarcoplasmic reticulum, where calcium ions are stored. It is the release of the calcium ions by the action potential that actually allows contraction to take place. The return of the calcium ions to the sarcoplasmic reticulum initiates the phase that we term "relaxation." Calcium ions, when released from the sarcoplasmic reticulum, bind with troponin, which then frees the myosin ATP-ase to convert ATP to ADP, allowing contraction.

· Another aspect of muscle physiology is the different types of muscle fibers. Much of the literature about muscle fiber types has led to a great deal of confusion. Approximately 5 years ago, six different systems of classification were used for muscle fiber types. Many of these were developed on animal models, and some of the fiber types discussed were

---

Jack Wilmore, PhD, is professor of physical education at the University of Arizona in Tucson, Arizona.

found to not be relevant or appropriate for the human. Recently, a system of classification has evolved that is almost universally accepted. Basically, there is the fast-twitch fiber, termed the FG fiber, that is quickly fatiguable. Also, there is the fast-twitch fiber that is fatigue-resistant (FOG), as well as the slow-twitch fiber, which is highly fatigue-resistant (S). Each of these, then, has definite characteristics allowing differentiation between types. For example, the actual contraction force in grams reveals that fast-twitch fatiguable fiber has a very high power output. The intermediate or FOG fiber does not exert nearly the same degree of force. The slow-twitch fiber, which is fatigue-resistant, has a very low force output. Thus, force ouput allows one to discriminate or distinguish between each of the three fiber types.

With respect to the fatiguability of muscle, the FG muscle fiber starts strong, but in 3 to 4 minutes it essentially reaches full exhaustion. The FOG fiber that has fatigue-resistant properties continues for a much longer period of time. Finally, the S fiber has the greatest degree of resistance to fatigue.

Another characteristic differentiating muscle fibers is the difference in the size of the fiber. The FG is the largest fiber, the FOG is intermediate in size, and the S fiber is very small; this has implications for various recruitment patterns. The muscle biopsy technique used to obtain muscle samples for studying the various characteristics of muscle and fiber types has been perfected to the point where individual fibers can be isolated. Much of this pioneering work is being conducted in Sweden and at Ball State University in Muncie, Indiana.

Strength has been more or less the hallmark of the field of physical education for close to a century, and yet we probably know less about the physiology of gains in strength than we do about any other area in the physiology of exercise. We have made the assumption that strength gains are the direct result of increases in the size of muscle. We know when we strength train an individual, the muscles become larger and the individual gets stronger. Therefore, we assume a cause-effect relationship. As the muscle gets larger, it is able to exert more force. Yet several studies on strength training with women have found essentially little or no change in the size of muscle, even though it doubles and sometimes even triples in strength.

From these and many other experiments, it is now recognized that the expression of strength is related to, but not dependent upon, the size of the muscle and is probably more related to the ability to recruit more muscle fibers in the contraction, or to better synchronize their contraction. A classic example of this is the woman who is washing the dishes at the kitchen sink. She looks out the window and sees her son working underneath his automobile. The jack slips and the car falls on top of him. She races out the door, lifts the car—which weighs some 3,000 to

4,000 pounds—off of him, and in the process shatters her vertebrae, ribs, and so on. But nevertheless, she is still able to lift that automobile off of her son. We also see examples in the sporting community. Bob Beaman's record in the long jump was nearly 2 feet further than anyone had ever gone before. Somehow he was able to recruit an inordinate number of muscle fibers or better synchronize their contraction in order to complete that record-breaking jump. You can imagine his inner frustration ever since that time. He must wonder, "How did I ever do it? How can I ever repeat that performance again?" He has never come close, nor has anyone else.

We have not begun to fully understand what allows a person to become stronger. One possibility exists, a theory that has been around for several years, concerning the motor neuron and its subsequent innervation. The motor unit has various impulses that impinge upon it, some of which are positive, some negative. We know, for example, that if two impulses come to the neuron simultaneously—one a negative impulse and the other a positive one—they cancel each other and the result is no contraction. With superhuman feats of strength, it is theorized that the body is somehow able to block or inhibit the inhibitory neurons, allowing for recruitment of a greater number of fibers. These inhibitory impulses serve, to some degree, to protect the body from tearing itself apart. And if athletes knew how to block their inhibitory impulses, they could literally tear their opponents apart.

There is a very sound basis for the neurological control of strength, which may help explain some of the phenomenal increases in strength shown with the electrical stimulation techniques used in the East German and Russian training centers. Several of these stimulators are available in the United States, and these may facilitate research that can better define the basic mechanisms of strength gains. It is imperative that we know how a muscle gets stronger, because only then can we develop efficient strength training programs. Today, we are still the victims of the equipment manufacturers.

Next, I would like to review strength testing techniques and then discuss the various modes of strength training. Isometric testing, a strength testing technique, was first introduced by Dr. Harrison Clarke. Dr. Clarke used the cable tension tensiometer, a technique he had modified from cable tension testing that had been conducted in the Air Force on cables used to secure airplanes. The Air Force tensiometer enabled researchers to test the actual amount of tension or force applied to the cables. Dr. Clarke's modification allowed isometric testing of various isolated muscle groups at specific joint angles.

Isotonic strength is most often tested by the one-repetition maximum procedure, where through trial and error one can identify the amount of weight an individual can lift just once. If the individual is able to lift it more than once, more weight is added. If he or she is not able to lift the initial weight, weight is subtracted. This technique is termed "one-repetition max," or "1-RM" and is widely used to test strength efficiently for large groups of people.

Isokinetic strength can be assessed using a simple isokinetic testing device such as the Mini Gym. This device has a dial that reads out the amount of force exerted; it is a crude measure but it can be used and modified. There are more accurate readout systems that can be attached to the Mini Gym equipment; these systems are expensive but can provide an accurate readout of the actual amount of force the individual is producing. The Cybex II is the best single mode for isokinetic testing today. Its two-channel recorder allows recording of both the joint angle in the range of motion as well as the actual torque at each angle. It is an expensive unit, and undoubtedly would break down with a great deal of use, making it undesirable as a training device.

Now, what are the different modes of strength training, the strengths and weaknesses of the various systems, and the possible problems when using one or more of these types of systems? First, isometric exercise has existed for quite some time, although interest in this form of exercise was rekindled in the 1950s, when Hettinger and Müeller in Germany initiated research in the area of isokinetics, observing the effects of a single 6-second contraction. Subsequent research modified the procedure considerably to maximize strength gains. Isometric training can be accomplished in various forms. For example, you can push against the doorway or push or pull against yourself, providing your own resistance. Isometric bar racks have been developed which provide much greater versatility. No actual movement of the joint angle occurs with this form of training, and one is able to perform a maximal contraction. Studies have shown isometric training procedures to be equivalent to isotonic training for gains in strength. The 5% gains in strength per week are remarkable, and this kind of training does not require expensive equipment. It is something that athletes can use as a take-home program, where they exercise in their spare time at night or on weekends. The program could also be used during the summertime or during the off-season conditioning period when the athletes are unsupervised.

There are inherent limitations to isometrics, however. The biggest single limitation of an isometric program is the lack of positive feedback about changes in levels of strength. When you push against a doorway, the doorway does not move, so you do not know if you are getting stronger. When you pick up a 50-pound weight and lift it over your head, you know you have lifted 50 pounds. If in 2 weeks, you can lift 60 pounds, you know your ability to perform that lift has increased by 10 pounds. Isometric exercises do not give that kind of feedback. To motivate people to perform, there must be some type of positive feedback for reinforcement. Another problem with isometrics is that the actual activity does not provide direct feedback; thus, it is easier for athletes who are not highly motivated to "gold brick" in this particular form of training, and the coach and trainer cannot determine whether they are contracting maximally.

Also, strength gain with isometrics is essentially limited to a narrow range in the total range of motion. It has been estimated that strength is gained at approximately plus or minus 20 degrees from the angle of training in the range of motion. For example, if an athlete is using an isometric bar, simulating a curl at 90 degrees, then he or she is increasing strength from approximately 70 degrees up through 110 degrees. The bar will have to be adjusted at three or four different locations in the range of motion in order to assure maximum strength gains through the full range of motion. Although isometric exercises will produce strength gains similar to those obtained with isotonic exercise, isometrics have declined in popularity because of the limitations inherent in them, mainly the lack of positive feedback. Isometrics are now used with patients who have a casted limb to help them maintain some degree of strength or tonus during the rehabilitation period.

Isotonic strength training, exemplified by freeweights, is the most widely used form of strength training in use today. There are inherent problems in using free weights, however, such as the problem of safety and potential injury. This has been somewhat eliminated by the use of the packaged systems like the original Universal Gym or Paramount systems, which place the weights in controlled stacks. The traditional weightlifter is typically not motivated by stacked weights, but the concept is ideal for the novice.

Isotonic weight training has developed largely by trial and error over the years. The original work of DeLorme and Watkins in the 1940s and the work which led to the development of the Oxford technique of the 50s were largely a matter of putting something together on the basis of logic and then building on it. The whole concept of three sets and the optimal number of repetitions per set essentially evolved from someone saying, "Well, maybe this is a good place to start." No one has modified that program much since. The original technique consisted of 100 repetitions performed over 10 sets and was later modified to 3 sets. The sequence was largely evaluated by trial and error. If strength training is anything like distance running, trial and error is approximately 3 to 4 years ahead of the researchers. With strength training, it is maybe 15 years ahead, because we know so little from the research. The athlete in the weight room everyday is experimenting in order to obtain maximum gains. Coaches and trainers are in ideal situations to experiment with their athletes, probably more so than the researcher in the laboratory who has limited access to subjects.

Isokinetic exercise has been a major breakthrough in strength training, having evolved over the past 12 years. Theoretically, isokinetic training offers a tremendous advantage over other traditional forms of strength training. A typical strength curve allows us to calculate the force an individual is able to produce at each point in the range of motion. In other words, in a curl-type movement with flexion of the elbow, the elbow flexors are at 100% of your strength at approximately a 90° angle. This simply means you are maximizing your strength at that particular point. As the angle decreases or increases from the 90°, the ability to generate force decreases. When athletes doing curls approach the point of fatigue, they typically "cheat" by not completing a full extension. They do so because they are at their weakest point in the range of motion at full extension, using only approximately 45% of their optimal strength. What this means in terms of weight training is that if athletes lift only 45% of their capacity at 90° in their initial starting position, they will be substantially below what they could lift at the strongest point in their range of motion.

From a theoretical standpoint, the inability to tax a muscle maximally throughout the range of motion imposes obvious limitations in the maximum gain of strength for that muscle throughout its full range of motion. Isokinetic devices allow maximum contraction at every point in the range of motion. As an illustration, go to a service station and put a car on a hoist. Place the hoist to the level where you can perform a standing press. As the hoist moves upward slowly, exert maximum force as if you are lifting the car. Obviously, you are doing very little to lift the car, probably contributing zero to the total force that is lifting the car. Yet, the car is continuing to move at a fixed speed. No matter how hard you push, whether you are 10 years old or a strong professional athlete, you are not going to be able to have any influence at all on how fast that car moves upward. At each point in the range of motion, however, you have been able to exert maximum force. Motivation is a big factor here and must be taken into consideration. But, theoretically, the potential exists for doing maximum contraction at each point in the range of motion. This means that you will be exerting less force initially than at midrange although you will be using the same percent of your maximum. So the definite inherent advantage is being able to tax the muscle equally throughout the full range of motion.

Accommodating resistance is the final form of strength training discussed here. Equipment is designed to vary the resistance to match the strength curve of each individual. This is done, for example, in the Nautilus equipment by the ingenious cam, which alters the mechanical advantage and changes the amount of resistance to which the individual must apply force in order to move the weight. This is the basic idea behind accommodating resistance: trying to match the resistance to the individual's strength curve. This means loading the athlete maximally at his or her strongest point in the range of motion, as well as loading the athlete maximally at his or her weakest point in the range of motion.

The strength training should be as specific to the sport as possible. That includes not only the motion, but also the speed at which the motion is completed. Again, this is one of the inherent advantages of truly isokinetic devices. In most isokinetic devices, the speed of movement can be varied from very slow to very fast speeds. One can maximize gains in strength and performance by approximating the speed of contraction used in the movement during the actual event. There is one very important factor related to "performance," however. We may have missed the boat in the past with strength training studies by evaluating improvement only on the basis of gains in strength. For example, if as a basketball coach I have my athletes perform an intensive strength training program, and I double their strength in the benchpress, curl, and leg press but observe absolutely no improvement in performance, this program was a waste of time. In other words, strength gains have absolutely no merit in and of themselves. Performance must be the bottom line.

Finally, when working with any highly skilled athletes, you must make sure that their performance is not negatively affected by the strength training program. With such athletes, you must always have a way to assess their performance in order to evaluate the usefulness of the strength training program.

Two other topics need mention: strength training for women and circuit weight training. Women, who typically are weak because they have been discouraged from using their upper bodies from an early age, basically enjoy strength training. Female upper body strength is about 30-50% of males', whereas lower body strength for men and women of similar weight is comparable. It is not unusual to see some women double their strength in a period of 10 to 12 weeks of strength training. Women were previously discouraged from strength training due to the fear of muscle hypertrophy. Although women do hypertrophy, the average female will not do so to the same extent as the male. There will be minimal gains in the size of muscle, perhaps a quarter of an inch over a 10-week period.

The final topic of discussion is circuit weight training. In our work with professional athletes, we became aware that off-season conditioning is a critical area that has received relatively little attention. Many athletes totally neglect or even abuse their bodies during the off season. Thus, an efficient off-season conditioning program is needed to keep these individuals in some semblance of fitness. When professional athletes complete 9 or 10 months of exhaustive workouts and games, they feel they need 2 months for complete rest. Such athletes need a program to maximize their conditioning in as short a time as possible. A primary interest here is cardiovascular conditioning. Can one obtain similar benefits with a circuit weight training program to those obtained with traditional circuit training? Are the changes in aerobic capacity comparable to the changes obtained from jogging programs? Are increases in strength comparable to a typical weight training program? Can flexibility be maintained? In a series of experiments, my colleagues and I found that individuals participating in an intense circuit weight training program were working at an average of 90-95% of their maximal heart rate, but at only 40-45% of their maximal oxygen uptake. Women, not men, increased in both cardiovascular endurance and flexibility, although this finding may have been due more to the motivation of subjects rather than to an inherent difference between the sexes. Changes in strength were not as large as those expected from a typical weight training program, but were nevertheless substantial. The same findings were observed with muscular endurance.

Generally, then, circuit weight training is a good form of exercise for off-season conditioning. It can be done in a confined space, it does not require a great deal of expensive equipment, and it can be completed in a 20-25 minute period of time. Also, such a program requires a commitment of only 3 days a week.

In summary, the whole area of strength development is extremely exciting. We have only a limited understanding of the area at this time, but we must strive to develop it. I am certain that for many athletes the secret to success in performance will be dictated by how well we can bring them to their potential relative to strength and power. For example, the better we understand distance running and those factors controlling distance running, the better we are able to train our athletes for more optimal performances. We need to develop that same degree of sophistication in the area of strength training. When we do that, I am convinced that we will see tremendous gains in strength, power, and athletic performance. And all of this will help good athletes become better.

Strength Training: Program Organization and Proper Neck Development

Dan Riley
The Pennsylvania State University

During the 1960s, weightlifters and bodybuilders were the primary source for strength training methods, and their techniques were handed down to coaches for years. Coaches relied primarily on information from these athletes because in the past they had feared possible adverse effects from a year-round weight training program. Once they recognized the value of such a program, they were forced to turn to the "experts" of that period, who were the only people with any real practical knowledge of how to get stronger and bigger muscles. So coaches and athletes adopted the lifting routines of the bodybuilder and weightlifter. A generation has passed, and athletes are now passing on these same methods to other athletes.

It is not difficult to gain strength. Anyone can do it using almost any technique available. Fortunately, better, more efficient methods are available for the trainer, coach, and athlete than those once learned from bodybuilders and weightlifters. Getting coaches and athletes to understand and accept some of this information, however, is difficult and often impossible. Coaches and athletes are practitioners by nature.

If another team (or athlete) is successful, coaches assume that whatever methods it uses must be the key to its success. The truth of the matter is whenever a team is more successful, it is because it has better athletes and is probably better coached. It is the responsibility of every professional to provide the athlete with a program that (a) produces the best results, (b) consumes the least amount of time, and (c) best prepares the athlete for competition. Strength training is an important part of the overall process of preparing an athlete for competition.

Dan Riley, MS, is strength coach at The Pennsylvania State University in University Park, Pennsylvania.

An athlete must make many important commitments to be a successful athlete. Therefore, we must re-evaluate our programs to ensure that our athletes are reaching their physical potential while taking the least amount of time to do so.

Neck Development: The Correct and Incorrect Approach

At Penn State, we have two rules we observe while developing the neck muscles.

Rule 1

Never exercise the neck muscles before a game or practice.

Rule 2

Never perform an isometric or static contraction for the neck muscles.

Common sense tells us that after a muscle is exercised (overloaded), it is not as strong as it was before it was exercised. The muscle will also fatigue faster than if it were not exercised prior to an activity. Neck-strengthening exercises before a game or practice are both illogical and unjustifiable. Yet most major college and pro teams perform all kinds of exercises for the neck before a game or practice. This exercise may be just enough to fatigue the neck muscles and leave them more vulnerable to injury than if they were not exercised before. Therefore, stretch the muscles before a game or practice and exercise them after.

We have our second rule (i.e., no isometrics) simply because there are too many better alternatives to isometric exercise. If flexibility of the muscles is to be maintained and strength maximally developed throughout the full range of movement, the muscles must be exercised throughout their full range. Isometric exercise, when compared to isotonic exercise, is assuredly an inferior mode of training.

A neck flexion exercise, neck extension, and lateral flexion left and right exercise can be performed manually. Manual resistance is a form of resistance exercise designed to maximally improve muscle strength and endurance. Manual resistance can be applied by one athlete while the other performs the neck flexion and neck extension exercise. Self-imposed manual resistance can be applied by the lifter while performing the lateral flexion exercise to the right and left.

The trainer and coach must spend some time showing athletes how to develop the skills to perform these exercises before exposing them to the methods used. The skill required by the spotter and the lifter to safely and effectively perform the exercise is a major limitation of manual resistance. One of its many advantages, however, is that no equipment is needed. Also, with this method a large group of athletes can be trained at once. During the season, a lack of equipment and time usually prohibits most teams from maintaining and developing additional neck strength, and this obviously leaves athletes more susceptible to injury.

Manual resistance is not just an alternative; if properly performed, these exercises can be more productive than anything available. Unfortunately, too few coaches or trainers are willing to learn how to properly perform them. Too often, too much is lost in the interpretation. This is a disservice to the athlete. Trainers with a neck machine should by all means use it. Otherwise, they should learn to properly perform the available manual resistance exercises.

Performing Exercises Properly

Overloading the muscles makes them stronger. Remember that the goal of an athletic trainer is to produce the best results in the least amount of time. Athletes will develop maximum gains in strength in the least amount of time while performing any isotonic exercise if proper attention is paid to the following five points:

1. The exercises must be full range;
2. The muscles must be allowed to raise the weight;
3. The lowering of the weight must be emphasized;
4. Athletes must exercise to the point of momentary muscular failure; and
5. All exercises must be supervised.

Full Range Exercise

Everyone agrees that a weight must be raised and lowered through the muscle's range of movement. The weight must be lowered at least through the muscle's existing range of movement to maintain and hopefully improve its flexibility.

Again, common sense dictates this, yet many athletes can be observed in the weight room sacrificing range of movement to make the exercise easier. Range of movement is often sacrificed at the expense of productive exercise to lift more weight or perform more reps.

Allow the Muscles to Raise the Weight

Athletes should eliminate the use of any fast or jerky movements when raising the weight. This allows the muscles to do the work. If any explosive or extremely fast movements are used, the weight is too light or some momentum is being used to raise it. Using momentum decreases the productivity of the exercise because it relies less on the muscles. Also, fast or jerky movements increase the chance of injury. Athletes can raise the weight as fast as they can or want, as long as the muscles are doing all of the work and the use of momentum is eliminated.

Emphasize the Lowering Phase

Any isotonic exercise has two phases: the raising phase and the lowering phase. The same muscle that raises a weight is also the same muscle used to lower it, so the lowering phase of an exercise can also produce strength gains. When athletes lower a weight slowly, they are resisting the gravity pulling the weight down. When athletes take a long time to lower a weight, as well as add more weight during this phase, they are overloading their muscles and thus building their strength. Athletes using conventional equipment should take 3-4 seconds to lower the weight.

Reach Momentary Muscular Failure

The two major factors in stimulating maximum gains in the least amount of time are *time* and *intensity*. Thus, the muscles must be exercised at the highest intensity for the correct amount of time.

The intensity is at 100% when the athlete fails momentarily, when he or she can no longer perform another repetition. It is difficult and almost impossible to measure intensity that is anything less than this. Therefore, athletes should continue exercising until they can no longer properly perform another rep.

The key is to select the proper amount of weight to allow the muscles to be exercised for the right amount of time to best develop the muscles for the activity involved. Because most athletes are involved in anaerobic activities (i.e., football, wrestling, lacrosse, gymnastics, field hockey, etc.), we recommend that the muscles be exercised for at least 40 seconds and not more than 70 seconds. These are just guidelines, however. If the exercise is performed using the guidelines outlined in the first three points, then the athlete should perform somewhere between 7 and 12 repetitions of each exercise. Most athletes reach their limit somewhere in that repetition range.

Emphasize Supervision

The above four points should not be performed unless each repetition of every exercise is supervised by a training partner. The major responsibilities of the training supervisor include the following:

1. Recording the weight used and reps performed for each exercise on a workout card. This will eliminate the duplication of a previous effort

and ensure progress.

2. Encouraging the lifter to stimulate an all-out effort.

3. Discouraging the lifter if he or she does not pay proper attention to points 1-4.

4. Dropping the weight or assisting the lifter if he or she cannot perform at least 10-12 reps. The lifter should be assisted only as much as is needed to complete 12 reps, and the supervisor should only record the reps the lifter properly performed alone.

In summary, the team physician and trainer can help change coaches' methods, who gleaned their knowledge from weightlifters and bodybuilders. As professionals, we athletic trainers must seek and utilize those methods that produce the best results in the least amount of time.

Obviously, changes need to be made for the benefit of the coaches and athletes. Although this will not happen overnight, perhaps the leadership of the NATA will stimulate changes and assist coaches in implementing these methods.

Nutrition in Children's Sports

Nathan J. Smith
University of Washington

Participation in sports is often an effective way of motivating children and adolescents to develop a high interest in many health matters including nutrition. The young boy or girl athlete soon becomes aware that what one eats and drinks largely determines a person's available energy and body composition, i.e., fatness, weight, etc. Knowing that energy and body composition affect one's athletic performance, the large number of youth who are becoming active in today's sports programs are therefore becoming concerned about their dietary practices. There is no better opportunity to upgrade nutritional habits than by counseling them on diet as it relates to athletic performance and health. A good diet can never make a champion out of a "klotz," but many a high-potential athlete has underperformed because he is either misinformed or uninformed about nutrition.

The Basic Diet and Avoidance of Supplements

The young athlete should know that intense physical activity, training, and athletic competition do not increase the need for specific nutrients, but do increase the body's energy and water requirements. In other words, the food intake necessary to satisfy the energy needs of the active

Nathan Smith, MD, is professor of pediatrics and orthopedics at the University of Washington in Seattle, Washington.

young athlete provides an optimal amount of the protein, vitamins, minerals, amino acids, etc., that the body requires (Mayer & Bullen, 1960). Thus, there is no place in the healthy athlete's diet for vitamin, protein, or mineral supplements that are so vigorously promoted to the uninformed, highly motivated, and vulnerable population of athletes.

The young athlete can best satisfy his or her nutritional needs with a varied diet taken as three or more meals a day. His food energy intake should be adequate to maintain a desired competing weight and to support growth. By eating at regular intervals throughout the day, he will be sure of having a steady supply of energy needed for vigorous exercise and to feel fit. The common practice among teenagers and young adults of eating a single meal late in the day, along with irregular snacks, cannot meet the energy needs of a training program, particularly when the practice sessions are held in the late afternoon.

A diet pattern that will maintain the desired body weight and include a sufficient intake of all essential nutrients is referred to as the athlete's "basic diet" (Smith, 1976a). To repeat such a diet makes protein and vitamin supplements unnecessary, wastefully expensive, as well as potentially dangerous. The athlete's basic diet need only be modified on special occasions to meet some very particular energy needs of different types of competition.

In counseling the young athlete regarding his basic diet, the physician may use the four or five-food group plan that most young people have been taught by the time they reach high school. The athlete can be assured that all of his or her needs for essential nutrients will be met with two servings of each of the dairy and high-protein groups of foods, four servings from the grain and cereal group, and four servings from the fruit and vegetable group every day. Depending on the foods selected, these 12 servings, if eaten in moderate portions, will provide only 1,200 to 1,500 kcal, an inadequate energy intake for any young athlete. Thus, the basic diet is one that ensures a good intake of essential nutrients, but to which second helpings and preference foods are added to satisfy energy needs. The active boy or girl can be reminded to "first eat what you need (the basic diet), then eat what you want."

This food group-based diet will not satisfy the iron requirements of 10 to 15% of the women athletes. The iron content of even a high-quality American diet and the limited ability of the body to absorb iron require that 1 in 10 normal healthy women regularly use a medicinal iron supplement.

The Benefits of Regular Intakes of Energy

The regular intake of energy throughout the day, as well as regularly throughout a training period, is essential in meeting the energy demands of very active athletes. The well-nourished high school boy who has reached near-adult size has no more than 1,200 to 1,400 kcal of readily available carbohydrate energy in various compartments of his body at any one time. This is only sufficient energy to meet the demands of less than 12 hours of sedentary schoolday activities. The individual who has missed breakfast and whose lunch has been a minimal snack or less will have inadequate energy to perform well during an afternoon training session. Regular meal-time eating three or more times a day provides a highly desirable food energy intake pattern for the athlete in training and competition. The all-too-popular eating pattern of one large evening meal and intermittent, irregular snacks during the day will often send the athlete into practice or competition seriously lacking in available energy.

Recent muscle biopsy studies reported by Costill and his co-workers have demonstrated how overtraining and limited food energy intake preceding competition can deprive the muscles of adequate reserves of glycogen, an important source of energy, and contribute to so-called "staleness." Distance runners training with long runs every day, even while following a generous diet of which 60% of the Calories were provided by carbohydrates, were shown to have progressively lower concentrations of muscle glycogen each day while training. A tapered training period of 3 or more days—in conjunction with a good diet was needed to replenish the glycogen stores and to optimize muscle energy available for competition. The results of these studies show the necessity for regular and continuing good food energy intake during training, and for the modification of the intense training schedule several days before important competitions, so that energy reserves are optimally replenished and preserved. The high-energy output athlete—i.e., the basketball player, the distance runner or swimmer, the soccer player, the cross-country skier, etc.—will do well to pay attention to his regular and continuing energy needs.

Optimal Energy for Different Sports

The serious boy or girl athlete will often benefit from informed advice on the best ways of meeting the specific energy needs of differing types of sports or competitions.

In certain athletic events of very short duration, such as the 50-yard dash, the pole-vault, certain types of gymnastic competitions, etc., the brief periods of competition are separated by significant rest periods. These contests involve short bursts of anaerobic energy supplied by ATP and phosphocreatine. In preparing for such contests, the athlete should be sure that his dietary intake for several days preceding the contest is good, that he maintains a proper level of hydration, and that he has a regular intake of high-carbohydrate liquids such as fruit juices, or light meals, so that ATP and phosphocreatine can be efficiently regenerated.

A good, regular fluid intake is essential and often difficult, particularly for female athletes. In the pressured environment of competition, thirst is not a reliable indicator of fluid needs. Scheduled intakes of water or very diluted fruit juice every 60 to 90 minutes are an effective way of providing adequate hydration. Commercially available electrolyte beverages are not recommended, since a diet that provides sufficient energy and generous intakes of cool, palatable water can satisfy the needs for fluid and various salts. Home-made mixtures are also not advised, since an error during their preparation may result in an unsavoury substance which will interfere with an adequate water intake. Again, the well-nourished and well-hydrated athlete does not need special preparations.

Contests that demand all-out efforts for periods of 3 to 10 minutes or longer, such as crew races, wrestling matches, middle-distance running and swimming races, all depend on a most demanding combination of aerobic and anaerobic energy metabolism. These sports are among the most difficult types of events to train for. Muscle glycogen storage contributes significantly as a major source of energy for these types of competition (Hulfman, 1967; Mathews & Fox, 1976).

Performance in competition requiring great endurance is improved by training and dietary programs that maximize the glycogen content of muscles. The modification of the basic diet to accomplish this end has been referred to as "glycogen loading." Muscle glycogen stores are maximized by first depleting the muscles of glycogen by limiting the carbohydrate intake during vigorous training workouts early in the week before a contest. Then, beginning 3 or 4 days before the event, the athlete supplements his basic diet with up to 1,000 to 1,500 kcal of carbohydrates in order to replenish and maximize muscle glycogen stores.

The above-described restriction in carbohydrate intake during the depletion of glycogen in the muscles is a demanding experience for the athlete and may interfere with his training schedule at the critical period of 3 to 5 days prior to important competition. However, the high intake of carbohydrates in the 3 to 4 days immediately before the contest will then result in maximal glycogen stores, and thus an optimal level of energy for performance.

Many athletes choose to avoid the period of severe glycogen depletion and heavy exercise, and to merely maintain a high-carbohydrate intake during the 3 to 4 days prior to important competitions. However, the glycogen content of the muscles under these circumstances has been demonstrated to be somewhat less than if the athlete had subjected himself to a period of glycogen depletion and carbohydrate restriction which may, in fact, be much more compatible with many training schedules.

It is important to emphasize that "glycogen loading" is designed only for the serious athlete preparing for important competition of appropriate duration. It is not recommended as a routine diet to be followed over a course of many weeks during a sports season. It does prepare the athlete optimally for the appropriate types of contest, and if he follows it, he is sure to avoid ill-advised dietary habits.

Wrestling and Other Weight Control Sports

Physicians in many states have been assigned by coaches and athletic associations the responsibility of certifying the high school and junior high school wrestler's competition weight. In other situations, parents seek physicians' advice about how participants in wrestling programs should practice weight control. A well-planned weight control program should be provided for the aspiring young wrestler so that starvation, dehydration, drug abuse, and a variety of other problems can be avoided. At the present time, as many as 200,000 American high school boys may be suffering many months of growth arrest during the wrestling season as they attempt to lose weight in order to participate in wrestling programs.

Several studies have documented a level of body fatness that represents an optimum ratio of muscle mass, strength, and endurance to body weight (Tscheng & Tipton, 1973). This optimal ratio will represent the desired competing weight for the young wrestler. How this level of body weight, i.e., body fatness, is achieved is of critical concern to the wrestler.

Over the past several years, a weight control program has been developed that can cut down on the abuses in high school wrestling programs and at the same time contribute to the education, fitness, and competitiveness of the participant (Smith, 1976b).

Soon after school starts in the fall, the potential members of the wrestling team are weighed and measured, and a maturity assessment is made. An estimate of the level of fatness is made using a skin fat fold caliper.

It is important to recognize that the average white male high school student from a middle or upper income family will have an excess of body fat. Recent population surveys suggest that as much as 15% of the body weight of the average white male living in an affluent family is body fat. Recent studies have demonstrated that 5% to 7% of body weight as body fat represents an optimal ratio of muscle mass and body strength to body weight. Thus, one might project a loss of 10% of body weight as body fat for a high-school boy with 15% of his body weight as body fat. Such a projected fat loss should ordinarily occur no more rapidly than 2 pounds per week. The wrestler's diet during this time should be a generous, basic diet from the four food groups, providing no less than 1,800 to 2,000 kcal a day. This would probably be some 500 to 700 kcal less than the athlete requires to maintain his weight. This modestly restricted caloric intake still allows three meals a day, but not desserts and in-between-meal eating. In addition, fat loss is promoted by encouraging the young athlete to increase his energy expenditure by at least 500 to 700 kcal each day. This will involve a general conditioning program that is prescribed by the coach, e.g., an hour or more of running, interval training, weight-lifting, etc. Weight reduction by an increased energy expenditure and only a moderate reduction in caloric intake will result in a loss of body fat in teenage boys and will not decrease lean body mass in the way that more restricted diets will do, and will not interfere with normal growth.

It is absolutely essential in such a program that weight control activities be started many weeks before the competing season begins in late November and December. Weight assignments for competition should make allowances for growth, and the entire weight control program should be supervised by someone other than the head wrestling coach. A trainer or assistant coach, or team physician will usually be most effective in the weight surveillance of the young wrestlers.

It is important that specific steps be taken to inform parents, school administrators, school nurses, and community physicians of the basis and validity of the wrestling team's weight control program. Likewise, it is essential that weight and fatness be carefully monitored on a weekly basis throughout the competing season, as there is a tendency towards a return to once-established levels of over-fatness.

Weight Gaining

There is considerable concern about the widely publicized abuses associated with weight reduction and weight control in high school and junior high school wrestling programs. Less well recognized but of no less concern are the nutritional abuses of weight gaining or "bulking up" by a large number of high school and junior high school-aged football players (Smith, 1976b). Without medical or nutritional guide-lines, hundreds of thousands of young men spend their spring and summer months attempting to gain 20 to 40 pounds of body weight on high-fat diets supplemented with a variety of useless and potentially dangerous vitamin, mineral, and protein supplements. This is nutritional abuse of the worst sort and is often compounded with the use of anabolic steroids and Periactin® . These drugs are ineffective, dangerous, their use is unethical, and they have no place in healthy conditioning programs.

American football is a popular sport that is attractive to many boys, large numbers of whom desire to increase their body weight in order to increase their playing potential. These young men need nutritional counseling by an informed professional who can assess their growth potential, as well as direct them to safe dietary practices and training routines.

In our experience, a typical 6-ft-tall, 165-lb. 16-year-old aspirant can gain 10 to 15 pounds of lean body mass and improve his potential as a football player if he works hard, if he is well disciplined, and if he can afford to provide the caloric intake needed to support this gain. The young athlete must recognize that if he is to increase only muscle mass and not become obese, then only muscle work and not any specific food, vitamin, or hormone will produce an increase in muscle tissue. Experiencing a weight gain of 1 to 2 pounds per week will require adding 500 to 1,000 kcal each day to his usual diet and doing 1 hour of heavy muscle training several times each week. Each pound of lean body mass gained represents a positive caloric balance of approximately 3,000 kcal. A weight gain of 1½ pounds per week is the maximum that one can anticipate if the increase in weight is to be limited to lean body tissue.

Throughout the period of potential weight gain, skin fat fold is repeatedly measured. An increase in skin fat fold will call for an immediate modification of the diet and the weight-gaining program, an increase in training, and a decrease in caloric intake until it is demonstrated that body fatness is not increasing.

The necessary increase in caloric intake can be best produced in weight-gaining programs by following fat-modified diets such as the American Heart Association Prudent Diet for American Males. This diet reduces the saturated fat and cholesterol intake by limiting the consumption of fatty meats and dairy products and can contribute positively to the nutritional education of every young man and his family. It is the only diet plan that we feel best regulates the increase in the caloric intake of the young athlete during his weight-gaining experience. If the athlete's family has a history of early cardiovascular disease, the family is referred for blood lipid studies and appropriate follow-up.

Iron Deficiency in the Athlete

Iron deficiency has been demonstrated to be a common problem, according to all recent nutritional surveys in the United States (Smith & Rios, 1974). There is likewise increasing evidence of significant functional limitations in physical and learning abilities associated with mild degrees of iron deficiency and iron depletion, both of which are unrelated to the presence or absence of any anemia. In any population of athletes, it is important to identify any one who may be suffering from iron depletion or iron deficiency. This becomes increasingly important as large numbers of girls and young women begin to participate in sports programs. There is rarely a problem in identifying individuals in sports programs who suffer from frank anemia as the result of a long-standing iron deficiency. The anemic individual is usually compromised to an extent which is unconducive to participation in high energy-expending sports. However, mild degrees of iron deficiency are common in high-risk populations and may significantly limit performance.

Several populations are at risk to a lack in iron. Women, who may be iron-depleted after the menarche, represent the largest group. In studies of a large Washington State population, there was very little difference in the frequency of iron deficiency among low and high-income teenage girls. Ten to 15% are found to have degrees of iron depletion detectable by biochemical tests such as transferrin saturation, plasma ferritin levels, or erythrocyte protoporphyrin concentrations. Less than half of these girls will have detectable anemia. Iron deficiency in males participating in sports programs is limited to adolescent boys who experience rapid adolescent growth on irregular and inadequate diets. This is most often encountered in populations living at the poverty level.

Recent experimental evidence suggests that mild degrees of iron deficiency, as recognized by biochemical assessments using protoporphyrin or ferritin measures may be associated with a limited ability (i.e., athletic ability) to perform physical work. The relatively low iron content of even a high-quality American diet, the limited ability of the human body to absorb dietary iron, the rapid rate of growth among today's youth living in affluent societies all combine to place many at risk to iron deficiency. An assessment of iron nutritional status is therefore highly desirable in the preparticipation health examination of all female athletes and of adolescent boys coming from backgrounds where their dietary intakes may be compromised, since an iron deficiency can significantly hamper an athlete's performance and motivation.

Pregame Meal

It is important to remember about demanding endurance-type contests that the Saturday match is played on Thursday and Friday's food intake. The pregame meal should not be looked upon as a significant energy source which must meet the needs of a high energy-demanding competition. The following guidelines should be considered in planning the pregame meal:

1. The meal should be a part of the emotional preparation of the athlete for the contest. The psychosocial aspects of food and eating can come into play, since mealtime is an opportunity for enhancing communication between coaches and team members.

2. The menu should include any food that the player feels may help his performance.

3. The meal should be low in fat, as fatty meals pass out of the stomach slowly.

4. The meal should be sufficient in amount so that the athlete is not hungry during the contest.

5. A modest contribution to energy needs can be provided by light, high-carbohydrate foods.

6. The foods that have an obvious high risk of transmitting food poisoning should be avoided (e.g., turkey, gravies, cream pastries, etc.)

The traditional pregame steak meal is high in fat content, leaves the stomach slowly, and should be eaten 5 to 6 hours before a contest. However, many players then become hungry during the competition. A much more desirable menu is one of fruit and juices or fruit punch, chicken and lean beef sandwiches, jello salad, sherbet, and cookies. This high-carbohydrate, low-fat meal can be taken 2½ to 3 hours before a game, and may, with minor modifications be made at home as a boxed or "brown-bagged" lunch by the low-budget athletic team. A similar menu is simple enough for the young athlete to prepare at home when no parent is around in the late afternoon to take part in meal preparation.

Complete liquid meals such as Ensure Plus® or similar products that have been originally developed for hospital use are finding increasing favor as pregame meals. They can be sipped in small amounts to within an hour or two of the competition. For those athletes whose anxieties are manifested in the gastrointestinal tract as they wait for the competition to begin, the complete liquid meal will help avoid pregame vomiting, as well as provide some fluid intake and a modest contribution of energy. These products may be used by some athletes as their only source of nutrition during day-long competition.

Tea with honey is a unique beverage combination that has considerable attraction for many young athletes. For the young participant who is not accustomed to caffeine drinks, a caffeine intolerance reaction may occur after a few cups of strong tea. A case of the "caffeine jitters" is highly undesirable during preparation for a contest. Large intakes of honey will leave the stomach slowly and may create some osmotic relationships, resulting in upper gastrointestinal distress and discomfort. Moderation is essential in all pregame food intake.

The Underfed Athlete

The team physician and the coach should be particularly alert to the nutritional status of the young athlete coming from a home in which there is insufficient food to meet the high food needs of an active young adolescent. Although an athletic experience may often be tragically overemphasized as young boys or girls coming from poor families, such an experience can enhance their self-image and may in fact be the only available avenue to post-high school education.

Nutritional surveys have repeatedly documented that poor families buy food of similar nutritional quality as do middle- and upper-income families, but for obvious economic reasons, they buy less. When food is limited in amount, the individual with the greatest needs, such as an active, growing, teen-aged athlete who participates in a high energy-expending sport such as basketball, soccer, etc., is at greatest risk.

The adolescent male athlete who comes from a poor family is at particular risk, since his stage of physical growth is associated with a large increase in lean body mass and thus increased nutritional needs. He may be commonly found to be iron deficient, but even more frequently, he will have an unpredictable and often inadequate energy intake. The appropriate steps to ensure an adequate dietary intake will often have a very significant impact on both the athletic and academic performances of these young boys or girls. It must be stressed, therefore, that the team physician and coach be especially concerned about the significant numbers of individuals whose athletic performance will be compromised by irregular and inadequate food intake.

Many physicians have become aware that large and rapidly increasing numbers of their young patients compete in sports programs. The young person's interest in athletic activities can be a very real factor in prompting him to become sufficiently concerned about good nutrition and health so that he can enjoy an optimal level of performance. Taking advantage of athletic participation as an opportunity to introduce young patients and their families to sound nutritional practices may well provide them with important lifelong health benefits.

References

HULTMAN, E. Physiologic role of muscle glycogen in man. *Air Res.* (Suppl.), 1967, **20**, 99-114.

MATHEWS, D.K., & Fox, E.L. *The physiologic basis of physical education and athletics.* Phladelphia: W.B. Saunders, 1976.

MAYER, J., & Bullen, B. Nutrition and athletic performance. *Physiological Reviews*, 1960, **40** 369-397.

SMITH, N.J. *Food for sport.* Palo Alto, CA: Bull, 1976. (a)

SMITH, N.J. Gaining and losing weight. *Journal of the American Medical Society*, 1976. (b)

SMITH, N.J., & Rios, F. Iron deficiency and iron metabolism. *Advances in Pediatrics*, 1974, **21**, 239-276.

TSCHENG, T., & Tipton, C. Iowa wrestling study. *Medicine and Science in Sports*, 1973, **5**, 1-10.

Salt, Water, and Athletes

Nathan J. Smith
University of Washington

Water, next to oxygen, is life's most essential substance and, as a nutrient, our most limiting and essential substance. Although the worldwide food crisis is the great tragedy of the 20th century, it is actually the world's shortage of water that most threatens the human race. We will die of thirst long before we die of hunger, and we will all probably go completely bats before either of these calamities occur.

Why is water so essential? How is it related to body function? All minerals, electrolytes, organic compounds, and gases are dissolved in water; most of the body's hundreds of biochemical reactions involved in energy metabolism go on in water; all transport functions are carried out in water; and of particular concern in relation to the athlete is that body heat is dissipated and transported by body water. Water, thus, is critical to a host of vital functions, and limiting the body's supply by inadequate hydration is one of the surest ways to compromise muscle function and athletic performance.

The body's relative water content decreases with age, particularly in

Figure 1—Percentage of water in common foods.

150

Table 1
Water Balance

72 kg Male			
Intake	Grams/Day	Output	Grams/Day
Water drunk	1300	Urinary water	1516
Water in food	800	Fecal water	24
Metabolic water	254	Insensible loss	800
	2354		2340

the young. The younger athlete, the little leaguer, has more body water and needs more water per unit body weight to meet his or her needs. Young athletes are also more vulnerable to water loss than adults.

Obese individuals have relatively less body water and a lower percentage of body water than do lean individuals. The obese, 200-pound guard may have no more body water than the lean, 166-pound flanker, an important point discussed later.

How is water balance maintained and what are the principal avenues of loss and intake of water? In an average sedentary male, there is an exchange of 2 to 2.5 liters of water (5 lb) each day. As we metabolize food, especially carbohydrates and fats, H_2O and CO_2 are formed, contributing to the body's water supply. The contribution made by water in food itself is of greater significance. The list of common foods and their water content shown in Figure 1 makes it apparent that a significant water intake results from eating fruits, vegetables, and even eggs. Although beverages are the major contributors, eating meals contributes significantly to meeting water needs. Consuming a sufficient amount of liquids is a problem area for many athletes, particularly young women. As shown in Table 1, control of urinary losses is the principal mechanism by which body water balance is maintained. The thirst mechanism is not very sensitive to changes in water balance and therefore less adequate for controlling the body's water balance. Urinary water losses will be influenced by water intake and by insensible water losses such as evaporation of water through lung and skin surfaces. Such losses vary greatly, influenced by metabolic activity, environmental temperature, humidity, wind velocity, and so on.

Water demands from exertion in the dry, moving air of high altitudes have not always been appreciated and have caused the failure of more than one mountain climbing expedition. An early Swiss attempt to conquer Mount Everest failed when the fuel allotment was limited so that only one pint of water a day was available during the final ascent. As the men became dehydrated, their energy failed.

Insensible water losses from lungs and skin are accentuated during jet air travel. The rapidly moving air, low humidity, and inaccessibility of significant quantities of water in the airplane make a transcontinental air trip a dehydrating experience. The consumption of alcohol and caffeine-containing beverages only accentuates the problem. For athletes traveling to an important competition, scheduling fluid intakes before and after the flight, avoiding caffeine, and allowing enough time to rehydrate at the end of a long air trip can contribute to performance.

How does exercise and competition influence water metabolism? Promptly after onset of vigorous exercise, plasma volume decreases, with plasma water moving to the intercellular space. As the metabolic activity concerned with energy production within muscle cells increases, in the presence of adequate water, lactate, potassium, and heat are transported out of muscle cells into intercellular water and plasma. Plasma water transports heat to the skin and lungs, where heat is dissipated through sweat and its evaporation.

Reduced plasma volume results in reduced renal blood flow, reduced glomerular filtration rate, and decreased urine production. Body water is thus conserved for intracellular metabolic activity in muscles and for sweat production. This sequence of events explains why water losses induced by environmental heat are different than those resulting from exercise. Experiments by Saltin and his colleagues revealed that water losses induced by heat came almost entirely from *extracellular* fluids rather than from *intracellular* water, as are the losses associated with exercise.

Under laboratory conditions a water loss of 1-2% of body weight will induce thirst. Under the intense conditions of competition or practice this is often far from true, so voluntary consumption of water in negative water balance becomes extremely important to the athlete. Under normal conditions, only ½ to ⅔ of water losses will be replaced by voluntary drinking, and without special provisions for correcting water deficits, 48-72 hours may be necessary to re-establish water balance after vigorous exercise. This phenomenon, called involuntary hypohydration, may be markedly accentuated by the athletes involved in intense activity and may compromise performance because of water deficit.

In studies at NASA, Greenleaf and his associates have studied these changes in great detail and have demonstrated that when diet is held constant, the rate of repayment of water debt is independent of the degree of water loss. The subject re-establishes base-line water content no faster after large than after small water losses.

The effects of hypohydration on well-trained athletes have been readily demonstrated with decreased work capacity after water losses of 2-3% of body weight. Wrestlers, for example, who must often "make weight," experience the negative effects of limiting hydration on performance; as little as 3 or 4 pounds of weight-cutting by a 140-pound wrestler can compromise performance.

Claremont and Costill documented a measurable effect on pulse rate and rectal temperature of subjects dehydrated by 3% of body weight from cycling for 2 hours. This undesirable change can be prevented by providing for anticipated water losses by "hyperhydration." With men given 750 to 1000 ml of water prior to exercising in high temperatures, the NASA group found lower pulse rates, lower rectal temperatures, higher sweat rates, and higher performance. This is due to maintaining the plasma volume, which can also be done by periodic intakes of water during exercise. Thus, drinking 12-16 ounces (1 ½ to 2 glasses) of water is advised before practice, and water should be available during practice as well.

Preventing and promptly replacing water losses is high priority in supporting energy metabolism and top performance of the high energy-demanding athlete. Handball, tennis, and squash players find this helpful during their 1- and 2-day tournaments. Water needs should be monitored by frequent weighings and weight maintained during competition.

Water should always be available; it should be cool, palatable, sanitary, and provided in generous amounts. The community water bucket and single dipper is too dirty, the plastic bottle is too little. In the intense environment of competition, drinking must be scheduled.

Compromising energy production by inadequate hydration can limit performance. More threatening is heat exhaustion, which is caused by the limited ability to transport and dissipate body heat when hydration is compromised. Plasma volume is inadequate to provide adequate blood flow to the skin and muscles and the central nervous system: The runner with low blood pressure and cold, pale, wet skin is the classic example of heat exhaustion.

Endurance distance events such as marathon running and bicycle racing in hot, humid weather demand good supplies of water to prevent potentially catastrophic heat disease. These athletes need adequate body water to transport metabolic heat to the skin and lungs and provide for sweating. Heat is lost from the body primarily through evaporative losses on the skin. The runner must be well hydrated, could run without a shirt on a hot day, and must have water available during a long, marathon-like event.

The American College of Sports Medicine (ACSM) has recently provided guidelines for prevention of heat disorders during long distance marathon runs. They are summarized in Table 1 and have been quite widely published. I would only warn against overenthusiasm for the electrolyte-glucose drinks and would recommend that those commercially available should be taken with at least an equal volume of cool water.

Serious, life-threatening heat disease is most commonly encountered during early football practices. Early practice typically involves obese, unconditioned athletes exercising vigorously in hot, humid weather with skin surfaces covered by 15 pounds of football uniform or even sweat suits. Mathews and Fox at Ohio State reviewed 12 high school and college football heat-stroke deaths and plotted the temperature and humidity at the time of death in nine of the deaths. Deaths occurred with both high temperature and low humidity and relatively low temperature and very high humidity. The heat that causes heat disease comes more from within than from without. Five athletes were not allowed water during practice and were required to take salt tablets; one wore a rubber sweat suit under his uniform and all were large, obese interior linemen.

If we recall that obese individuals have relatively less and actually no more body water than thin individuals, it is not so surprising that the obese, poorly conditioned lineman is at greatest risk. Insulated with large deposits of subcutaneous fat, covered with a full uniform, this athlete radiates heat poorly and has limited sweat evaporation. In a 2-hour practice, the lineman can lose 10 pounds of body water. Normal thirst response will prompt him to replace no more than 50% of his water deficit. The second practice session will result in repeated weight loss and limited replacement. Going into a third or fourth practice session, the lineman may begin with a 10- to 20-pound water deficit. Even though the day is relatively cool and the coach feels safe in pushing practice, in the middle of a hard practice the lineman may stop sweating, experience pounding headaches and chilliness, and collapse with a temperature of 106° to 108°. This is an emergency situation, in which the athlete must be immediately undressed, cooled, and taken to a hospital.

These catastrophies are preventable with appropriate action by the team physician and trainer and the cooperation of the coach. In the preparticipation exam, these individuals should be alert to factors that may place an athlete at risk, for example, obesity in the young, undermuscled, immature, and unconditioned boy making an attempt at football. Be sure athletes are well conditioned and acclimatized gradually. Keep good records of humidity and temperature, and make certain the athlete eats regularly. The most important preventative technique in early football season is weighing before and after each practice and comparing these two weights to detect accumulating water losses. Weight deficits of more than 3 or 4 pounds (2% body weight) require an increased water intake and excuse from practice.

Water breaks are necessary every 30 minutes in warm weather, with a clean, cool source of water available, and minimal uniforms are obviously desired. The uniform for the first week of practice in warm weather should be helmets, *white* t-shirts, and shorts.

The replacement of water is monitored by weighing, but salt (Na and K) losses are not readily quantified. Thus, there is considerable difference of opinion as to the amount of salt that should be provided. Personally, I believe athletes consume too much salt. An American diet will meet athletes' Na and K needs; this means that athletes should not miss meals. With large water losses of 8 to 12 pounds, some additional salt has been recommended, but only with massive water intake. Salt without water immobilizes intercellular water, removes water from within cells, and contributes to fatigue and heat disease.

The Gator-Aide-like drinks have concentrations of sugar and electrolytes that can reduce their movement out of the stomach. These beverages are expensive and contribute nothing regular meals and drinking clean, cool water won't provide. Home-made sugar electrolyte mixtures often are unpalatable and discourage adequate water intakes, and errors are likewise possible.

The closer the athlete's beverage is to water, the closer it comes to meeting the athlete's needs. Good nutrition for athletes, then, means water—and plenty of it.

PART FOUR

LIABILITY AND MANAGEMENT

Liability, Athletic Equipment, and the Athletic Trainer

Richard Black
Black, Robertshaw, Frederick, Copple & Wright

Liability

Several years ago, some judges and law school professors decided that the doctrine of negligence was no longer valid. They developed a doctrine of strict liability for products sold. I want to discuss, briefly, this concept's meaning and its relevance. The doctrine states that the company which *sells* a product is strictly liable to anyone who is injured by that product if that injury was a result of the product being "defective." Product liability means that if a store owner sells a can of beans with a microbe in it that he or she had no way of detecting and the consumer gets food poisoning, the injured person can sue the grocery store owner.

Philosophically, this social doctrine of the law has entered the area of football helmets. Because the doctrine of strict liability leaves the football manufacturers unprotected, we are faced with the serious risk of football exiting.

Suppose a helmet manufacturer sells a football helmet and a boy wearing that helmet sustains a head or neck injury. If the helmet is in exactly the same condition as the day it came off the manufacturer's table, it could be ruled as unreasonably dangerous and defective because it was not designed to protect this boy from a blow that could conceivably occur to him on the football field. With this reasoning, all of the helmets in the world are defective and unreasonably dangerous. This is the position of the plaintiff's bar that deals in this area, and the manufacturer or sporting goods dealer who sells that product is strictly liable in tort. This

---

Richard Black is an attorney in Phoenix, Arizona.

is the theory of law; this is what is happening and this is the danger of the sport.

The standards of liability for athletic trainers and coaches are fortunately different than those for manufacturers or sellers of equipment. The criteria for the sale of a product in strict liability is that the manufacturer must be an "A+" student. The athletic trainer and coach fortunately must be only "C" students, who must conduct themselves reasonably, ordinarily, and prudently. The standard is that of ordinary care under the circumstances to comply with the mainstream of what is done by the ordinary athletic trainer or "C" student. The problem is, however, that no one knows exactly what these standards are. Therefore, it is crucial that each organization develop standards of conduct giving guidelines with which to comply in case a suit goes to court. These standards will enable you to show that you complied. If a federal law applies to the entire country, you must comply with it. If a state law applies to you in your particular field of endeavor, whether it be athletic training or selling products or whatever, you must comply with it. If you do not comply with the standard, you are liable in court. If there is a city standard or a school standard, you cannot use your own rules; you must comply with the city or school standards. This is true for federal and state standards as well.

The National Operating Committee for Safety in Athletic Equipment has developed a standard that football helmets must meet in order to be used in colleges and high schools. Using and complying to NOCSAE standards can be crucial, especially in a lawsuit. NAIRS data, like the NOCSAE is also vital, for it provides accurate data on athletics. NAIRS should be expanded; it could provide trainers with statistical information of the merits of such things as equipment and food based on national surveys. Only athletic trainers, who are the most objective and knowledgeable people on this subject, should collect this data. Legally, the combination of NAIRS and NOCSAE could protect a school or trainer in a liability suit. A trainer's ability to say that he or she has used a NOCSAE product and can prove it with data from NAIRS can mean the difference between a guilty and a not guilty verdict. Although the standards themselves might not be good, standards and licensing can provide a quality measure. If licensing, procedures, requirements, and tests are met, it gives the school a boost in a lawsuit.

The Football Helmet

The 1978 issue of *Trial Magazine* included an article entitled "Product Liability," in which they address the football helmet as currently manufactured as dangerously defective for several reasons. They state that the face guard extends too far from the helmet, and that impact to the guard transmits the force rather than absorbing it, transmitting the force to the cervical area. Also, they claim that the rear, unpadded edge of the helmet is too close to the unprotected neck area, possibly allowing the rear of the helmet to be snapped down on the upper spine.

The fact is however, that it is not possible for the neck to be hyperextended by the back rim of the helmet. The Department of Transportation investigators and engineers have films which conclusively prove that in severe whiplash cases with automobile accidents, if you are hit from the rear, your head extends all the way and strikes your back at the thoracic area, then flexes forward and your chin strikes your sternum. With severe whiplash, the anterior ligament in front of the throat and soft tissue is torn, causing the injury. Although there may be some small fractures to the anterior portion of the vertebrae when the ligament tears away from the bone, no one has been able to find in any of these cases dislocations of the vertebrae and traumatized spinal cords, even when the head extended completely and touched the back. Countless films with football players, video-taped fluroscopes, have shown the same thing. Therefore, *Trial Magazine*'s theory of liability is totally inaccurate.

Frankly, the helmet is made to protect the head, not the neck. When a 200-pound football player, who has participated in strength and nutrition programs, puts his neck in a fixed position and strikes something, all the compression that the neck can allow occurs. The head stops on contact and the helmet protects the head (skull fractures in football have become rare), but the player's body keeps going. There is not enough padding in the world to alleviate 200 pounds of force from the body. Although a Florida court has ruled that a helmet should have a cut-out and padding in the back to prevent this kind of neck injury, neck injury can occur with any helmet because it does not occur by the back of the ring.

In none of the cases in which the plaintiff's lawyers have claimed that the rim of the helmet came down and dislocated the neck has there been found one bruise or mark on the back of the neck. They have suggested that the back rim of the helmet hits with such force as to smash through the ligament, and the flavum—one of the toughest ligaments in the body—and pushes through the spinous processes, without fracturing any of the processes or even causing a bruise. If the neck is hyperextended and all the facets are in the right position, they will not be able to get to the other side without a fracture. If the head is slightly flexed, however, and particularly if it is rotated and the blow occurs, the neck sits hard instead of returning. With the neck in this flexed position, the facets move up, allowing them to buck and go right across.

In addition, the football helmet cannot protect the neck from subdura hematoma injury if the force producing this injury is rotational acceleration. Force placed on the face mask, by rotational acceleration, can cause neck injuries. According to Allan Bernstein, it would take approximately 11 inches of padding on each side of the helmet to limit or stop rotational acceleration.

What you can do as a trainer to prevent injuries, then, is to never let yourself participate in or be part of modifying a football helmet so that it is different than before. First of all, it no longer complies with NOCSAE, and second, it makes you and your school liable if the player is hurt in that helmet. The changes made to helmets—particularly at the high school level—are amazing: Padding is removed, poorly fitting padding inserted, and screws are inserted with the sharp ends exposed. This problem is overwhelming. Thus, if you allow a player to wear an altered helmet, and the player is hurt regardless of the change, you and your school can be legally responsible. In only two football helmet cases was the defendant successfully defended.

Trainers must also be sure that coaches do not put a player with an obvious injury in a game. They must meet with the athletic director to develop written rules that determine the person with the authority. For example, if the team physician or the athletic trainer says a player is not ready to play and notes it on a written slip, the coach must comply and keep the player out. Programs without proper medical supervision, and authority to enforce it, are treading on thin ice.

We need to organize all the athletic trainers and prepare a presentation on what the football helmet can and cannot do. This would allow the athletic trainers to supervise that presentation. The coach does not want to do it, believing the presentation will scare the kids. We must emphasize to both athletes and coaches that the helmet must not be used for illegal tactics. Several dangers can occur if players violate the rules; for instance, a player can ram a tight-end in the kidneys with the top of his helmet to make him drop the ball, succeed, and paralyze himself for the rest of his life. The coaches should be made to understand that if they do not allow this to be told to their kids, they are likely to be selling vacuum cleaners in 5 years. Frankly, football may not exist because there may be no helmet manufacturers left. For example, Ridell, a football helmet manufacturer, has an insurance policy with a deductible of one million dollars.

Who has the professional objectivity to see that this message is in fact conveyed and explained and understood by all the players at the blessing of the athletic director? The athletic trainer. If it becomes household knowledge to every football player what the real risks of playing are, it will soon become household knowledge to the parents and to the country as well. The high school players emulate the pros when they talk about sticking them and putting their heads down, but the pros do not have rules against spearing. They have better conditioning and better physical structure, but they are not immune.

Summary

NOCSAE is vitally important because it provides a standard, and NAIRS is vitally needed for providing the information on the gray areas of sports participation. These allow trainers to know about many phases of athletics, about what works and what does not work—information about nutrition or athletic shoes—for injury reduction. All of these areas are vitally important. Let us realize what the football helmet can and cannot do and make it known to all of our players. Understanding your NAIRS data because it may win a law suit is secondary; you should use it because it will prevent athletes from being injured. Knowing the best equipment and how to use it properly reduces injuries. If players comply with the rules and understand that they must not butt, ram, or spear, it will reduce injuries. They must know that if they stick their head in the pile, they could break their neck. This responsibility is the athletic trainers', who are the most responsible professionals to handle this huge task.

Managing Your Medical Resources:
An Opportunity for the
National Athletic Trainers Association

Roger W. Hite
Mercy Hospital

Athletic trainers are in the health care business—and like those in health care delivery, they also should assume an active role in reshaping the system so it more effectively meets the health care needs of the people it serves. But how can athletic trainers, who have for so long been outside of the traditional health care system, accomplish this task? The following scenario may help to clarify the direction athletic trainers must take.

Some Definitional Issues

First, let's assume that I am in the unlikely position of athletic training program director at a local college and responsible for evaluating the quality of the existing program for educating athletic trainers. To add an element of drama, let's assume that a not-so-friendly dean is pressuring me to justify the program. For example, the dean believes that an athletic training program is undesirable unless it can be well integrated into the other medical ancillary training programs. The dean also believes that the athletic training program is simplistic, that it is an easy major providing the illusion of academic status for jocks, and that it only teaches jocks how to wrap the ankles of other jocks. The dean does acknowledge, though, that such a program has a limited social value inasmuch as it provides vocational opportunities for jocks who have exhausted their athletic eligibility. So, what can I do to make my program acceptable to the dean?

Such a scenario does not do justice to the problems faced by athletic trainers in their own programs, but it raises some issues that continue to

Roger Hite, PhD, is director of planning at Mercy General Hospital in Sacramento, California.

plague the athletic trainer's professional image within the university and in the traditional medical community. To overcome this inappropriate stereotype and to link both themselves and their programs more effectively with other medical resources, trainers should begin by realizing that they should raise their profile and make the substance and skills of their profession more widely acknowledged in the traditional medical community. The desire to learn more effective ways to manage medical resouces implies the awareness of a gap—a communication gap—between athletic trainers and other medical professionals, including physicians. What, however, was the factor that may have contributed to the gap between athletic training and the more traditional medical resources in the first place?

First, the value structure of the traditional medical practitioners is inherently different from that of athletic trainers. In many ways, athletic training seems antithetical to traditional medicine, for its goal is to apply the principles and methods of science, biology, physiology, nutrition, and so on toward the maintenance of health and the pursuit of physical and athletic excellence. The goal of medicine, by contrast, is to intervene in a condition of sickness, not of wellness. The traditional medical approach is not to help patients achieve levels of excellence in health, but to restore a sick body to an acceptable norm where there is absence of sickness. Only recently has medicine attempted to deal with the concept of "holistic care," a term for care that emphasizes wellness and the coordinated use of all information and medical resources that share this common value. The value of holistic medicine and emphasis on wellness has long been fundamental to the philosophy of athletic training, yet unfortunately, professionals in this field have not been in the forefront of bringing this value to the traditional medical community. Now that the wellness value is becoming widespread in the health care field, what will be the effect on the field of athletic training? It would seem to set the stage for remarkable growth and development for athletic trainers—if they are willing to assert themselves outside the university and academic setting. The emphasis on holistic care provides a commonground for communicating with other medical resouces—a commonground that did not exist a decade ago.

In addition to having a different value system, athletic trainers also have been virtually living in another world. Most probably live and practice in a world of youth, a university environment where everyone is plagued, it seems, by the illusion of immortality. Their contact is with the young, healthy, school age students who are seeking, through athletics, excellence and personal growth and development. Most athletic trainers probably spend proportionately less time working with nonuniversity-based older athletes, participating in a system which writes off this group and assumes they can be treated in the same category as all the other aging, sick, and unhealthy people. Unfortunately, until these "other athletes" have a serious problem and seek out a medical doctor, their medical and training needs go unmet.

I once conducted a series of interviews with our medical staff to ascertain their attitudes toward different potential programs for the hospital. While interviewing one of the young orthopedists, I asked him how often he dealt with athletic injuries. He replied, "It's difficult to have sympathy for a patient who cannot run more than 5 miles without pain when you see so many who are struggling just to regain the ability to walk!" I personally would not want to have advice about running and training from someone who, because of professional priorities, cannot relate to my personal needs to achieve wellness through injury-free running. This is not a comment on the physician's competence or mannerisms; the point I am making is that physicians simply don't have the time to cope with the problems of the wellness achievers. Although in the past this was not much of a problem, the recent upsurge in such athletes is going to create a strain on the traditional practices of medicine.

The definition of "athlete" may have also kept athletic training apart from other medical resources. What is an athlete? Is an athletic trainer's responsibility discharged once a person completes their athletic eligibility and/or leaves the academic setting? Doing so may have once been easy, because in past decades athletes tended to retreat from athletic competition and sports after their college years. Today, some remarkable changes in our societal values have created a new class of "other athletes"—people who devote a share of their lifetime energy to serious pursuits of athletic excellence. Certainly, what was once called the "running fad" has now become normative. Without question, the number of "other athletes" far exceeds the number of people currently encompassed by university-based athletic programs. Therefore, there is no better time for athletic trainers to consider how to manage this new group than now. How athletic trainers define themselves in terms of this newly emerging category of athletes will greatly influence their relationship with the established medical system.

Other definitional issues may also prevent optimum communication between trainers and other professional health care providers. Athletic trainers should view their profession as a bona fide medical resource. This may raise the eyebrows of those who wish to preserve a purist's definition that distinguishes practicing medicine—whatever this means— and practicing the skills and techniques of athletic training. This willingness to treat as separate and special the role of the physician has cost us dearly in our efforts to develop a well-managed health care system. It has created an unrealistic demand—and unrealizable self-expectations— on those in the medical profession. It has resulted, too, in economically rewarding a high status position which focuses on curing sick people.

The practitioner who helps healthy people get healthier receives no reward.

The sooner a health care system evolves in which realistic expectations, responsibilities, and authority are more equally distributed, the sooner a more rational, and presumably more responsive, system will exist. Athletic trainers can begin to reshape the system by viewing medical doctors as colleagues who share a common goal, or at least, who *should* share a common goal. When legitimate conflict arises over role definitions, trainers must not approach such conflict with an attitude that gives someone special consideration simply because s/he is a medical doctor, for to do so is to be self-defeating in one's efforts to relate professionally with medical doctors.

It is unfortunate but common that most people provide physicians with verbal and nonverbal cues which allow them to feel more comfortable in a superior-subordinate relationship. In effect, this creates a set of expectations for physicians that become self-fulfilling prophecies. Trainers will greatly enhance their communications with most physicians—and make the process a lot more comfortable for both parties—if they can learn to be assertive in their professional roles.

The term "sports medicine" is another wedge between the athletic training and medical professions. Although the term is widely used and accepted among university-based practitioners and researchers, and although it is an accurate description of what trainers do, the term raises a red flag within the traditional medical community. Many non-university-based physicians—primarily private practitioners—react to the concept of "sports medicine" as though it were an encroachment on their profession by quasi-professionals. Many view it as a continued fragmentation of the medical field that has already been too subdivided.

In addition, trainers need to market themselves as providers of medical services. Alternate labels for the sports medicine product can be easily found, and practitioners in this field will receive less resistance to change from the private medical practitioner if the term sports medicine is avoided because practitioners seem to view "sports medicine" as some kind of "fad" or "flaky" professional label. In most communities, then, there are few places for the other athletes to turn for medical information necessary to maintain their wellness goals.

Some Positive Actions

Now, if all the above problems were taken care of—that is, athletic trainers had a good definition of their athletic training program, were sensitive to the need to view themselves as colleagues of all other medical care providers, and were willing to avoid labeling their program "sports medicine"—what could be done to improve relations with other medical resources? What steps should be taken to integrate the field of athletic training into the mainstream of medical health care? First, an Advisory Committee of Medical Practitioners, which would advise and work with the athletic training program to assure its integration into the comprehensive medical care system, should be formulated. Such an advisory group could provide medical consultation to athletic trainers, lecture information for the classroom setting, and advice on new directions and growth for the athletic training program.

In addition to establishing a medical advisory committee, trainers should tap the resources available in the local acute care hospitals, beginning by establishing rapport with the physical therapy department. One way to begin might be volunteering to provide lecture information as a part of the weekly in-service educational meetings for the physical therapy staff, who would be delighted to have athletic trainers as a resource. A good relationship with the physical therapists provides a natural link to community orthopedists, rehabilitation medicine physicians, and other medical specialists who share a common interest in training and therapy techniques. The contact with physical therapy departments is useful in arranging jobs for students as physical therapy aides, which is a nice way to obtain part-time, on-the-job experience in a related field. And the physical therapists themselves can be a useful medical resource for athletic training programs.

Another way for trainers to establish communications with these medical resources is by linking themselves with the staff development and in-service education departments of the larger acute care hospitals in the community. These hospitals usually have a wealth of training aids, films and other visual aids, library resources, and access to countless medical educators. They can be very useful in helping to line up physicians to serve on panels and advisory committees. Most physicians have their own slide show and are usually generous with their time when it comes to talking about their pet research projects or some aspect of their field of medicine where they are especially involved as practitioners and researchers.

If the staff development connection fails as a link to medical resources, the next resource to turn to is the hospital's director of medical education. Usually, this role is filled by a physician who is responsible for coordinating educational symposiums and conferences for the hospital's medical staff. Those interested in participating in these educational conferences should make arrangements through this individual.

The county medical society is not the best contact for athletic trainers, because it tends to be a political debating society and deals with the organizational problems of the medical profession. These societies often have access to computer medical archives research systems, however, and the reference librarian can determine if this service can be made available to you and your graduate students.

Athletic training programs could also benefit from establishing communications with local cardiac exercise rehabilitation programs. Such programs are cropping up in communities throughout the country, and the physicians and technicians sponsoring these programs might be quite receptive to working with athletic training programs—especially because the application of exercise techniques in cardiac rehabilitation is a relatively new, developing field that appears eager to experiment with new techniques and procedures. Not only would there be some interesting potential for professional exchange between the trainers and physicians, but athletic training students might be able to serve intern roles as assistants.

One of the more neglected aspects of traditional medicine is the whole field of rehabilitative medicine. Athletic trainers who live in an area where such programs exist should contact the program director and explore ways they and their students could assist on both a volunteer and professional basis. A growth in the field of rehabilitative sports medicine in the next decade is not unlikely, and there is no reason why athletic trainers could not expand into this much-needed and neglected aspect of health care.

Linking with Primary Care and HMOs

As mentioned earlier, the "other athlete" group of nonuniversity-based athletes will continue to grow tremendously. Athletic trainers should pursue two strategies to capture a large portion of this market. First, they should recognize that everything in the health care field tends to point to the need to develop less in-patient acute care services, and to emphasize instead more ambulatory outpatient services. Traditional health care is having to change its purpose and mission statement; hospitals must now view themselves as a collection of health care services, not simply four walls and beds. Therefore, more hospital- and nonhospital-based primary care clinics will become available. The purpose of such services will be to reduce the misuse and abuse of expensive emergency services by people who do not have primary physicians, but who have third party payers such as the government, who will pick up the tab for emergency room treatment, even if the care is nonemergent. When these primary care clinics develop, they will take on a variety of shapes and organizational structures. They will be staffed by both physicians and ancillary medical professionals. It would be possible, desirable, and highly attractive in some communities to add an athletic training component to this setting. It makes especially good sense to have such a program hospital based because of the referral potential for other ancillary services and for hospitalization if such were indicated. An athletic training component to such a program would not be expensive and might be supported by an institution as a potential loss leader because of its referral potential and public relations possibilities. Establishing such a program in conjunction with your athletic training program would provide a new vocational career in the athletic training profession. Future students in athletic training will be looking for career opportunities outside the traditional academic-based athletic training programs.

In addition to joining primary care clinics, trainers should explore the possibilities of developing an athletic training component for a health maintenance program. The federal government is currently working to encourage the development of alternatives to the traditional fee-for-service medical care system, which requires patients—or their insurance companies—to pay each time they visit a physician for specific services provided. The government wishes to have more prepaid health care systems—called Health Maintenance Organizations (HMO)—to serve the total health care needs of patients. The philosophy of the HMO is to emphasize preventative medicine. Usually, the HMO enrolls participants, often through employer contracts, and charges a monthly premium for health care coverage, regardless of the amount of use by the enrollee. Some programs require that patients see a specific physician, others require that they select among doctors at a specific clinic, and still others allow patients to go to their own private physician, providing the physician has agreed to participate in the health maintenance system. In a sense, it is an insurance risk pool which prospers not when enrollees get sick, but when it manages to keep its enrollees healthy. Usually, there is great emphasis on screening and early diagnosis of disease to avoid advanced treatments, lengthy hospitalizations, and expensive surgical interventions. In the future, the HMOs will undoubtedly be fiercely competitive to enroll clients, especially the kind of wellness-oriented clientele that would be attracted to athletic training services. Indeed, many HMOs are currently looking at the possibility of providing executive fitness health screening and health care programs. To find new ways to relate to the mainstream of health care, athletic trainers should approach the HMO organizers with a proposal for developing a cost-effective athletic and sports medicine component for their program.

Effective Communications

Let's return to the subject of effective communications with the medical profession. People have a rather difficult time feeling comfortable in their interaction with a medical doctor, and the problem stems not so much from any communication problems related to the physician's interpersonal style—indeed, most physicians I know are genuinely good, sensitive people. The barrier to effective interaction is a systemic problem. Health care organizations have created a climate of expectation and given the doctor the role of a deity. The physician is the decision-maker who is only too aware of the medical and legal consequences of not living up to the expectation of infallibility in decision-making. It should be understandable, therefore, that much of the conflict that arises between physicians and staff can be traced to situations and circumstances where there is some ambiguity of responsibility. The medical role prescribed by us for physicians makes it difficult to delegate responsibility and to share the decision-making process. Even in situations where it is mandatory that the physician rely on the observation and analytical abilities of a highly trained staff nurse to provide information essential to the physician's decision-making responsibility, it must be clearly understood that any decision is the physician's. The nurses who have the best rapport with physicians seem to be those who respect the realities of the medical system, which dictates that the physician must have the final authority and ultimate responsibility. The strategy is to have a clear understanding of one's responsibilities to the patient and to the physician. It is no longer possible for the physician to simply view his or her ancillary personnel as incidental to the medical treatment of the patient; nurses and other medical technicians do much more than comfort the patient. The technician has expertise the physician must rely upon, and the technician's role will not diminish in the evolution of health care. Athletic trainers working with a physician, then, should certainly want to be perceived in the same light as other ancillary medical specialists. Athletic trainers having difficulties "communicating" with physicians should probably consider the problem their own and stems from their own lack of self-confidence and assertiveness. If assertiveness is the problem, then trainers should look into the assertiveness literature and programs designed to assist nursing personnel improve their interpersonal relations with physicians.

The best way to improve communications with anyone is to develop a broader basis of commonality. How many trainers know which physicians in the community are active athletically? How many are runners? How many play tennis or racquetball? Knowing which physicians are athletes and being able to acknowledge their athletic achievement can go a long way toward developing a commonground for building stronger professional rapport. For example, in many communities physicians organize athletic teams in a variety of sports. It wouldn't hurt for athletic trainers or their students to work with these teams as trainers.

Other Resources

I have tended to focus on the medical doctor as the primary medical resource; this is a limited perspective, however. The local acute care hospital is literally a gold mine of medical resources. The dieticians in the dietary department, for example, can provide information about nutrition or work with an athletic training department to develop nutritional programs for athletes. A good working relationship with the pulmonary medicine programs at local hospitals is beneficial, especially for doing blood-gas and pulmonary function testing on athletes. Athletic trainers could gain access to experts and equipment at reasonable costs if they cultivate professional ties with the director of respiratory medicine. Pharmacists are some of the most highly trained, and under-utilized, experts in the health care system. Most hospital-based pharmacists, especially those who have a commitment to education, would be flattered and eager to work with athletic training programs. In addition, most hospitals are interested in having their organizations viewed as a community clearing house for health-related educational information. With the increase in hospital-sponsored educational community forums, the services of the athletic training personnel will be highly valued.

In summary, the business of helping people maintain high levels of wellness should be a comprehensive team effort. The trend in health care planning is to better integrate the diverse resources into a more unified and effective health care system. It is costly and ineffective to continue to isolate so many professionally overlapping resources. I would hope that as health care services are redesigned into a system that is more responsive to the needs of people to maintain wellness, athletic trainers will give greater consideration to how best to get into the mainstream. I would hope, too, that athletic training and sports medicine will soon be available to the "other athletes" at a cost they can afford and in a system easily accessible to them.

DATE DUE